THE ART OF
UNIVERSITY TEACHING

Edited by

George Melnyk *and*
Christine Mason Sutherland

The Art of University Teaching
© George Melnyk & Christine
Mason Sutherland 2011

Library and Archives Canada
Cataloguing in Publication

The art of university teaching /
[edited by] George Melnyk and
Christine Mason Sutherland.

Includes bibliographical references.
ISBN 978-1-55059-411-9

1. College teaching.
I. Melnyk, George
II. Sutherland, Christine Mason

LB2331.A76 2011
378.1'25   C2011-903742-4

ISBN 978-1-55059-411-9
E-Pub 978-1-55059-425-6
SAN 113-0234

Cover design: James Dangerous

We acknowledge the support of the
Government of Canada through
the Canada Books Program for
our publishing program

Canada

Also acknowledged is the financial
assistance of the Government of
Alberta, Multimedia Development
fund for the support of our
publishing program.

We are grateful for the financial
assistance of the Faculty of
Arts and the Department of
Communication and Culture,
University of Calgary.

Detselig Enterprises Ltd.

210 1220 Kensington Rd NW
Calgary, Alberta   T2N 3P5
www.temerondetselig.com
temeron@telusplanet.net
p. 403-283-0900 f. 403-283-6947

To All Those Who
Have Taught Us Well

Table of Contents

The University

FOREWORD

Much is Expected From Those to Whom Much is Given

Karim-Aly Kassam

TEACHING IS THE *RAISON D'ÊTRE* of scholarship, because it provides a context for sharing insights gained through applied research. While publication of research brings validation by peers, teaching ensures engagement with those insights into the future. Conversation and exchange through teaching produce a dynamic that allows ideas to develop and hybridize into a tapestry of possibilities. Despite increasingly market conceptions of universities, students are not just 'consumers' of information, they are 'producers' of insight. As Kuhn noted in *The Structure of Scientific Revolutions* (1996), paradigm shifts generally emerge from (1) young scholars and (2) from those outside a discipline. This acknowledgement of the role of the young scholar in contributing to knowledge speaks to the fundamental role in advancing ideas. In short, teaching matters for the advancement of knowledge.

Furthermore, the culture of interdisciplinary thinking high-lighted in this collection acknowledges that the problems faced by societies and communities rarely present themselves neatly or in reference to a single discipline. Issues of poverty, sociocultural and environmental change, and food security depend on multifaceted responses and draw upon a diversity of approaches. By building bridges across different ways of knowing, teachers and students draw from the diversity of their cultural backgrounds and variety of life and learning experiences.

As teachers, our challenge is to make book learning at university relevant to societal needs. It is the role of the teacher to develop a pedagogical framework which facilitates transformation of students from those who know *about* major challenges of the 21st century to those who know *how* to engage these challenges in a particular socio-cultural and ecological context. It is the role of the teacher to combine a historical sense with relevance. To place an issue in context, students must consider not only the "pastness" of the past, but also its presence: that is, by analyzing an issue through historical reflection in combination with its relevance in the present and exploration of future possibilities. The idea of relevance links education to experience and learning to community. By combining critical thinking and practice, the student experiences how theoretical perspectives both emerge from and inform the applied context. By combining critical thinking and practice, the student experiences how theoretical perspectives both emerge from and inform the applied context. In the process of this type of learning, the particular hints at the universal (Jacob 1982), where broader meaning emerges from specific understanding.

Such a perspective on teaching seeks to generate a cadre of young scholars who situate their thinking and ideas in the context of a universe-centered self rather than a self-centered universe. Fundamentally, rights such as freedom are intimately linked to responsibilities that are associated with those rights. The notion that much is expected from those to whom much is given arises not from the vocabulary of the market economy, where a debt is owed to society, but from something much deeper. Barber (1994) argued, "The language of citizenship suggests that self-interests are always embedded in communities of action and that in serving neighbours, one also serves oneself" (p. 88). Self-interest does not exist outside of community but arises from engagement with the community from within. A conversation about learning that does not include practice is just as vacant as a discussion of rights without responsibilities. Responsibility is embedded in knowledge as well as in rights. To educate without causing students to reflect on consequences is tantamount to making machines out of humans, alienating students from themselves, their community, and their ecology (Kassam 2010).

This book is as much an ode to teaching as it is to the students that make up the vibrant classrooms and lively engagements that occur within them. It is being written at a time of change, when the interdisciplinary culture of the Faculty of Communication and Culture at the University of Calgary is being absorbed into a wider administrative infrastructure and where teaching and research are increasingly seen as distinct activities, despite a modicum of lip-service to the inherent linkage between the two. Finally, it is being written at a time when humanity collectively faces an environmental crisis, an energy crisis, and an economic crisis simultaneously. There are no models or approaches in place to deal with this triumvirate of challenges. The best hope is the next generation, our students. Therefore, this ode to teaching is not only a recognition of its role in learning but it is also a plea for thoughtful education policy.

References

Barber, B. R. (1994) 'A proposal for mandatory citizen education and community service', *Michigan Journal of Community Service Learning* 1. 86–93.

Jacob, F. (1982) *The Possible and the Actual.* Seattle, WA. University of Washington Press.

Kassam, Karim-Aly. 2010. 'Practical Wisdom and Ethical Awareness through Student Experiences of Development,' *Development in Practice,* 20(2); 205-218.

Kuhn, T. S. (1996) *The Structure of Scientific Revolutions.* Chicago. University of Chicago Press. (Original work published 1962).

INTRODUCTION

George Melnyk
& Christine Mason Sutherland

I N RECENT YEARS, a small group of colleagues in the Faculty of Communication and Culture at the University of Calgary would meet for an hour on Wednesdays to discuss ideas. They wanted to get to know each other's thinking about intellectual issues and so grow out of the stressful isolation of research and teaching that is common among academics today. University teachers tend to act like independent contractors involved in their own universes rather than cohesive and engaged groups of employees. This meeting was an act of affirmation, a mode of resistance to the corporate thinking that was taking over the university. Sometimes an article would be the basis for discussion, while at other times we would speak freely on public matters. The group was expressing a different sense of collegiality than the official one tied to committee work. It was meant to be a periodic exercise in congenial intellectual discussion in which we hoped to learn from and about each other as scholars and thinkers. One of the recurring themes in our meetings was the state of teaching in the university. On the one hand, we all enjoyed teaching and cared deeply about our students. On the other, we could not ignore the fact that over the years teaching had been increasingly devalued by the academic hierarchy. It is this deep concern for teaching and the problems that beset it that has given rise to this book. As participants in the group the editors of this book view it as a way of carrying on these noon-hour discussions in the same spirit of informality and conviviality.

The collection expresses a range of views on the teaching experience in the university and it is meant to stimulate reflection by professors and students. The book addresses a widespread dissatisfaction, a disease that has been growing over many years among frontline academics about the valuation and application of teaching techniques. At the same time, it is meant to celebrate our teaching, to take delight in students and their achievements.

All the contributors have taught or studied – sometimes both – in the former Faculty of Communication and Culture, now part of the Faculty of Arts at the University of Calgary as the Department of Communication and Culture. The Faculty of Communication and Culture was a special place that prided itself on interdisciplinarity and teaching. The Faculty had been named General Studies at one time, and part of its mission was to integrate all first-year students into university life. Later on, the Faculty re-branded itself as Communication and Culture. Most of the contributors to this collection have studied or taught in other faculties at the University of Calgary, as well as in other universities in Canada and beyond. Most of us are not scholars in education as such: we speak as practitioners, drawing on our own experiences. It is important for practitioners to make their voices heard so that those embarking on a career of university teaching as well as those who are already engaged in it will see the kind of energy and sound values teaching requires.

The essays in this collection are organized into three sections. The first section comprises discussion of the experience of teaching from the point of view of the teacher: what teaching is and how it can be approached. The second section deals with teaching from the experience of the taught. Beginning with a detailed discussion of what characterizes students today, it also includes two essays, one from a recent graduate and one from a graduate student in programme. The third section is concerned with philosophical reflections on teaching, its history and the changes it is undergoing in the Digital Age.

We begin with multiple-winner of the University of Calgary's Teaching Award, Ronald Glasberg, whose essay is based on the "Lecture of a Lifetime: Good Conversations As the Goad to Joy," that he gave at the invitation of the University of Calgary Senate in April 2009. Glasberg sees himself as enormously privileged to have a job that he enjoys so much. For Glasberg, one of the most important responsibilities of a teacher is to conduct and inspire the exchange of ideas between the instructor and the students and also among the students themselves. It is his aim to challenge the passivity with which so many students listen to their lecturers, to stimulate them to engage actively with ideas, even to disagree and argue with him. Such active engagement, he believes, will help them not only to learn but also to mature as human beings and to contribute to their world. He considers the classroom as a site for a good conversation and all that a true conversation implies, including joy.

Christine Mason Sutherland's autobiographical essay shows how the experience of being taught helped her to understand the importance of relationships between teacher and students. She gives an account of her long experience of education from both sides of the lectern, starting with her memories of being taught in a village school in wartime England. She sees the development of a corporately structured university as compromising these relationships, and she suggests changes in certain practices that might restore the centrality of teaching. For her, the student experience should not be compromised by bureaucratic agendas. It should lead to intellectual liberation and personal maturity.

Margo Husby discusses her passionate commitment to teaching derived in part from her experience as a student. For Husby, teaching is a way of being, a matter of who we are rather than what we do. Teaching is not static but generative, and like all living things, constantly changing. Husby describes her own gradual recognition of her vocation to be a university teacher by recalling the professors who encouraged her, the staff who supported her and the students who inspired her. But she also discusses the difficulties of working in an institution that values and rewards research above teaching. She favours a holistic approach to teaching that can deal with different aspects of the human personality.

Brian Rusted draws on his own experiences to show how performance can bring to life what is learned in the classroom. Education, he believes, has too often been disembodied, too purely cerebral, and unrelated to the life style and background of the students themselves. Most traditional educational theories and practices have been developed by the elites of the world, and are only marginally relevant to the marginalized. They are usually embedded within a print culture that does not take seriously alternative ways of knowing. Rusted wants to promote a lived experience of the meaning of what is learned, a personal engagement of the bodies and minds of the students with their own concerns and projects. One of the ways of achieving this kind of holistic education is through performance.

The perspective of committed professors needs to be evaluated by those who are meant to benefit from the teaching – the students. The second section highlights their perspective, but it begins with a powerful academic study profiling today's student and the impact of digital technology on their expectations and needs.

The essay from Jo-Anne André offers an illuminating analysis of today's "millennial students," who are in many ways different from those of the eighties and nineties. Coming from sheltered, even affluent homes, they have high expectations of success and a strong sense of entitlement, believing that effort, rather than achievement, should be rewarded by high grades. Not only the teaching staff but also administrators are challenged by these new expectations and demands. In the contemporary climate of competition for student enrolment, they are putting more of their resources into student services, and less into instruction. André gives some alarming figures about the depletion of funding for the teaching professoriate.

Cooper H. Langford teaches students how scientific knowledge and technological innovations interact with society and so change the cultural and intellectual temper of the times. He is a proponent of the "discovery" approach to scientific studies because it leaves "a long-term residue" of understanding with the student. He also believes that undergraduate students can be integrated into research programs. As an interdisciplinary scholar who bridges the divides between science, the liberal arts and the social sciences, Langford has a sociological understanding of the role of science in society, which he considers crucial for students in both Science and Arts faculties.

James Butler, who is completing his PhD dissertation, celebrates the interdisciplinary approach that he experienced as both an undergraduate and a graduate student in the former Faculty of Communication and Culture. He begins by distinguishing education from training, calling education "transformative." For Butler, it has been. His immersion in interdisciplinary models of learning and research has changed him by offering new insights into the experience of others, be they scholars with different approaches or other cultures in the world who offer real challenges to the meaning and value of research to them. Butler considers it a moral obligation for researchers to give back to the people they study, acknowledging the changes they bring about by their mere presence. They must try to ensure that the results of such study are constructive for the people studied as well as for the researcher.

Dalmy Baez gives a telling account of her experience as an undergraduate, from her earliest days of bewilderment to her final year as President of the Students' Union at the University of Calgary. She traces her progress, showing how the courses she took and the teachers she encountered helped to form her and move her towards maturity. She explains how what she learned in the classroom came to be applied to her responsibilities outside it in unexpected ways. The skills she gained at the university became the cornerstone of her professional identity.

The continuum from student to teacher and back to student provides the framework for the third section. It begins with Dawn Johnston's essay, which, like Butler's, celebrates interdisciplinarity. Johnston's joy in teaching grew from her experience as a graduate student in the Faculty of Communication and Culture, where she first learned about interdisciplinarity, and where she found teachers who, instead of competing, cooperated with one another to give her the best possible supervision. She has drawn on this positive experience in her capacity as Director of Students, whose role it was to nurture and support incoming students during their first year. Although this position was cancelled when the Faculty of Communication and Culture became absorbed in the new Faculty of Arts in 2010, Johnston translated her commitment to students to the classroom, where she continues to include individual student paths in the learning process.

Doug Brent believes that a research university ought to take responsibility for teaching undergraduate students how to do research. They should not have to wait until towards the end their studies, the senior seminar, or even graduate school: from their very first days in the institution they ought to be made to feel part of a community of scholars. Working alongside the teacher and drawing on the expertise of the librarian, they can learn not only the basic principles of research but also the enjoyment and the sense of achievement that it can bring.

Teachers also dream dreams and see visions. George Melnyk's essay explores the nature of such dreams, fantasy courses that he will never teach, but that in some way contribute to the teacher that he is. It is this capacity to look beyond the classroom, beyond the immediate context or routine possibility, that keeps teaching alive. Even if the fantasy course is never taught, it recognizes the teacher's openness to new ideas, new approaches, and new methods. Dreams of courses that reflect a teacher's deepest interest in communicating insights keep academics flexible, open to change, and not constrained by utilitarian goals of profitability or "relevance."

The collection ends with Michael McMordie's reflections upon his long career as teacher, researcher, and administrator in universities both in Canada and in Europe. Informed by a deep and extensive knowledge of the history of western universities, McMordie's essay gives an overview of the differing trends in post-secondary education since the Second World War, as well as a stringent critique of more recent developments. He believes that universities have lost their way and have become increasingly subservient to a visionless pursuit of material wealth. His wisdom brings a timely warning to us all.

While the university as an institution evolves through the expansion of knowledge and public discourse about its role, the university teacher remains the carrier of both tradition and innovation. The university teacher maintains a perilous balance in trying to communicate both facets of learning to students. Teaching has always been a complex role and teachers have always been challenged by innumerable pressures and changing mores. Yet the belief in dialogue, or what Glasberg terms "a good conversation" remains at the core of those committed to teaching as a crucial academic pursuit.

THE TEACHER.

The Lecture of a Lifetime
Good Conversations As The 'Goad To Joy'

Ron Glasberg

I HAVE ALWAYS ENDEAVORED TO MAKE MY LECTURES *discussions or conversations. No matter how large the audience, my goal was, and still is, to draw individual members away from the passive stance that tends to accompany this form of academic interchange. Not only do I want to talk to them, not only do I want them to talk to each other, I also want them to talk to the authors whom I am attempting to bring to life in my presentations. It is in that sense that my lectures are all about good conversations.*

The late Randy Pausch of Carnegie-Mellon is most associated with "the lecture of a lifetime" concept — a lecture that is meant to sum up the life of a professor who is deemed to have a message of import to the wider academic community. In the case of Professor Pausch, who was challenged by what proved to be a fatal cancer, the message resonated with the world at large as it circulated first on 'You Tube' before it found its way into print (The Last Lecture). It was probably in the sense of seeking to inspire its students and faculty that the Senate of the University of Calgary sponsored its "Lecture of a Lifetime" series, beginning in 2008, of which this was the second.

* This essay in a modified form was originally presented in the "Lecture of a Lifetime" to the University of Calgary community on April 16, 2009 under the sponsorship of the U of C Senate. The video of the lecture is available at the University of Calgary website. *www.ucalgary.ca/senate.*

In their desire to create and transmit knowledge, academics often forget the importance of inspiration – of bringing out the passion that should always accompany a love of learning and a commitment to seeking truth. When students make their often weary way to university in search of enhancing employment opportunities, and when administrators push the university into serving such needs while neglecting more fundamental goals, the ideals of authentic education tend to fall by the wayside. It seems sad when students go through their entire university career without once being inspired, and it borders on the tragic when they are totally unaware that they might have missed something in the process.

What follows is an attempt to sum up my career as a university educator by showing how having good conversations can inspire students, can goad them to feelings of joy that go hand in hand, not only with the pursuit of truth as an object 'out there in the world', but also with building those frameworks of understanding that bring us all together. A good conversation, among other things, is one that creates new perspectives, and a beautiful creation inspires all who partake of it.

THE WORD I WOULD USE to summarize my life as a university teacher is 'privileged', which is embarrassing because most people, even in a country as blessed as Canada, would not think of their lives as privileged. No small number of people look forward to the weekend because they hate what they have to do to earn a living. I, on the other hand, do not long for the day after Friday. I look forward to Monday as a time when I can return to reading good books and having interesting conversations with students and sometimes even with my fellow professors. Naturally all this makes me feel guilty. It is hard to enjoy the good life when most of those around you are experiencing a life of stress, strain, and general tedium.

At a recent meeting of my faculty, someone pointed out that the general public has no clear idea of what it is that academics really do, much less why it should support their activities with hard-earned tax dollars. Would it not add insult to injury to tell the public that the tax money they generate by doing unpleasant jobs is funding a life of joy for those who have the privilege of working as academics in publicly funded universities? I have to consider how my life of good conversations might be justified to an unruly mob making their angry way up University Drive. My sufferings with a top-heavy university bureaucracy and hours of marking barely literate student essays aside, I need to create an apology or justification for the bounteous benefits of my position. This essay is a kind of apology in the sense of justification for a very privileged life.

Apologia pro vita mea
or the metaphysics of conversation

THE FOCUS OF MY LIVING A PRIVILEGED LIFE comes from having good conversations. The context of good conversations is the humanities – the study of philosophy, literature, history, and the like. While good conversations no doubt occur in the hard sciences such as physics and chemistry – the bedrock of knowledge in our technological society – the public rightly perceives science students as being subjected to a rigorous discipline rather than having what appear to be esoteric conversations circling about unanswerable questions such as the meaning of life.

Good conversations refer to discussions about life, love, beauty, truth, wisdom, freedom, etc. These conversations are thoughtful and informed meditations and interpretations of 'classic' texts. A classic text is not just some great book in the sense that a group of academics have arbitrarily defined it as such. A classic text is one that articulates the most profound issues of life in such a way that their intricacies are not only revealed, but also presented in a manner that *inspires* those who read it to engage in an ongoing discussion of its central themes.

A classic text is an articulation of the fundamental assumptions by which we co-create the world. This is not some magical conceit, but an acknowledgment that our perceptions of reality are mediated by the conversations we have regarding the nature of reality, including how those very 'perceptions' and 'conversations' may be part of that complex of meaning. The categories by which we divide up the world arise in the context of an ongoing conversation that constitutes the evolution of our culture. In that sense different cultural conversations may be said to generate different realities. Whether these realities overlap or exist in isolation from each other depends on the progress of conversations between speakers who choose to learn about each other's cultural assumptions in what might be called an inter-cultural conversation.

Those who think my position here is over subjective, and at odds with the more objective stance that appears to characterize the hard sciences, would do well to consider scientific discourse as a kind of conversation itself – a conversation with nature via observation and experiment, but inevitably a conversation with other human beings who are together working out a categorical structure for the understanding of nature. Moreover, discussions need not be focused on the external world. Some hold conversations with what might be called higher forms of consciousness – higher forms often identified as 'God' – and in so doing have laid down the ethical or religious foundations of certain civilizations. Should one disagree with my take on science and religion, that disagreement is itself part of a conversation.

Conversations centered on classic texts bring participants as close as possible to the place where the world was and is being continuously co-created by ongoing discussions focused on fundamental cultural assumptions. If students develop a familiarity or facility with respect to this deep level of discourse, they may approach a position where they can re-create the world through new conversations informed by how earlier ones were instrumental in framing the contours of reality.

Should one still be skeptical with respect to the world-creative power of conversations, a good example is provided by the phenomenon of dreaming. Here we have what might be called an intra-personal discourse where one's unconscious mind and consciousness hold a kind of conversation, thus generating a dream-world. Until one wakes up, that dream-world is usually taken for reality. In the waking state the conversation shifts from the intra-personal dream to inter-personal reality. While it is an open question as to whether or not one 'wakes up' from that inter-personal realm, the world we take for granted derives its sense of being real from a conversational consensus that is developed over time. As that consensus changes, so does what is taken for the 'real'. However, the consensus is not without its disputed areas. Those who hold positions that cannot be integrated into accepted frameworks may be classified as mentally incompetent or even deemed to be evil and segregated accordingly. Should a conversational consensus become problematic in the context of various historical upheavals, the sense of reality arising from it may become disjointed. In other words, the fabric of reality may be rent with fissures and take on a surrealistic tone reminiscent of Kafka's nightmare world.

We converse; therefore we have a world. When we discuss fundamentals we co-create our world. If we can accept that conversations play a significant role in the construction of reality, then it stands to reason that good conversations will lead to a better reality than do bad ones. The question then becomes: "What is a good conversation?"

The 'Crisis' Of Public Conversation:
From Bad to Good Conversations

THE WORD 'CRISIS' IS PERHAPS one of the most over-used terms in academic discourse. However, when it comes to considering the state of public discourse or conversation, I believe the expression is more than apt. Before one can consider what good conversation may be, it is appropriate to cast an eye on what currently passes for conversation in the realm of public debate – the so-called cornerstone of democracy. Here one may observe a lack of faith in the very possibility of conversation and – what is worse – a lack of awareness about that lack of faith.

The first and more narrow example that I want to use concerns an editorial in the March 28, 2009, edition of *The Calgary Herald* in which editorial writer Lorne Gunter attacked the public funding of the CBC (Canadian Broadcasting Corporation) on the grounds of its liberal bias. He asserted that tax dollars should not be used to support the CBC's slanted views any more than to support a Christian outlet. Regardless of what one might think of Gunter's position on this question, it bespeaks a total lack of faith in the possibility of any group rising above its prejudices. For Gunter, it would seem that conversation is limited to one party endlessly repeating or reiterating its views to those who have not yet taken sides or to those, in some other group, who have not yet seen the light. Is that all there is? Can political conversation be reduced to endless repetition of one aspect of the consensus in some futile struggle for power – an aspect that takes itself as the only valid interpretation of the public good?

A second and wider example has political implications, but ultimately concerns the nature of reality. I am referring to the current attack on religion by such figures as Daniel Dennett, Christopher Hitchens, Sam Harris and Richard Dawkins. What these polemicists seem to forget is that religion is not just an abstract set of beliefs. It exists as a conversational bond between members of religious communities and this bond may include higher forms of consciousness associated with divinity. Do those attacking religion as irrational think that all religious individuals are feeble-minded, stupid, immature, ignorant, insane, weak, or evil? What choice do the die-hard attackers have but to make such attributions? But once one has painted members of the criticized group in such colors, possibilities for conversation have been reduced to nothing. If any of the attackers of religion met a religious individual whom they could not, in good conscience, call feeble-minded, stupid, immature, ignorant, insane, weak or evil, they would be forced to conclude that such a person had some kind of connection to what is real. Furthermore, they would then need to acknowledge that an open and honest conversation is called for, even at the cost of reformulating some fundamental cultural assumption central to the scientific world-view.

While many intellectuals do avoid exclusionary forms of discourse, polemical positions pertaining to politics, religion, philosophy, and science are not uncommon. Indeed, the existence of political parties with strangely intransigent positions points to a kind of failure of discourse that no one seems to find troubling. One would think that basic curiosity would push individuals to engage in conversations with those who, showing no signs of madness, stupidity, or malice, hold strongly differing views as to the nature of reality. One would think that such a crisis in discourse is unthinkable. Yet the foregoing observations indicate a basic ignorance about what a good conversation might be.

Surely we can do better than to endlessly reiterate rigidly held world-views in what passes for public discourse. The editorial position of any major newspaper is a case in point. No matter what the political stripe of the newspaper in question – left, right, or center – repetitive reiteration seems to characterize the editorial page. Few, if any, complain in their letters to the editor that the writers of opinion pieces are merely repeating themselves – something which indicates to me that the general public is as comfortable with discursive stagnation as are the makers, shapers, and articulators of public opinion. Whatever good conversations are, they have to be more than exercises in the reinforcement or refinement of one's prejudices.

If both parties to a dispute have expanded their perspectives, have let their outlooks be challenged, and have entertained new ways of considering the fundamental questions of life, then I would say the discussion has been worthwhile. Why? Because both parties have grown in the course of such a conversation, and one would think that growth is better than stagnation.

With the criterion of personal growth in mind, we are now in a position to consider in some detail the indicators of good and bad conversations. Specifically we can lay out a set of dichotomies that, on the basis of common sense, are designed to guide those who would have good conversations and help them to avoid having bad ones.

(i) Depth versus Superficiality:

A CONVERSATION CAN HARDLY FACILITATE GROWTH if it stays on the surface. By that I mean a good conversation has to go to the assumptions that underlie differing positions. Only when these assumptions are raised from whatever psychological depths in which they are residing can they become the subject of discussion. While this may be a painful process since personal assumptions are intimately connected with one's sense of self, this kind of pain promises a real gain in insight.

Let us imagine what this might mean in a concrete conversation. After hours of arguing, the parties to a dispute might reach the point where all they do to justify their respective (albeit conflicting) positions is to assert that each comes from some gut feeling about the world and how it works. The depth begins precisely at this point – the point where these gut feelings are explored and possibly transcended. For what is growth but the transcending of such foundational attitudes to the world?

(ii) Exploratory Boundary Breaching versus Defensive Boundary Maintenance:

APART FROM DIGGING INTO THE DEPTHS of a dispute, a good conversation should be ready to explore alternatives, to look at a problem in new ways, to breach what I would call the boundaries that have confined conversation to old ways of thinking. Boundary maintenance is a mark of bad conversation because it seeks only to reinforce an old pattern. While this might be acceptable if new approaches have been fairly considered, it can degenerate into a kind of mindless defensiveness when there is an intransigent opposition to any alternatives.

As one might expect, discursive boundary maintenance is closely linked to the maintenance of political power where challenging the complex relations between those who dominate and those who are dominated can destabilize a whole society. Little wonder that even the dominated might hesitate to move in the dangerous direction of breaching old boundaries if such could bring bloodshed upon their heads. Yet, conversation can only be corrupted by allowing visions of potential horror to hobble the imagination. It is ultimately human imagination that empowers the exploratory impulse to consider ways of avoiding the worst and realizing the best.

(iii) Courageously Creative versus Fearfully Tedious:

EXPLORING THE NEW brings to the forefront the next aspect of good conversation – namely, the creativity that goes beyond exploration and endeavors to come up with integrative overviews which unite differing world-views or outlooks. One needs to explore, but one also needs to work with those who are committed to old perspectives. Too often bad conversation finds a way of justifying the elimination of those who will not follow or commit themselves to the principles of some new order. Moreover, the creativity should come, not only from those who espouse the new, but also from those who hold to the old. After all, the co-creation of a world is a joint project, and commitment to what is being created can only be enhanced by encouraging an attitude of inclusiveness.

Naturally all of this requires courage – courage on the part of all participants in the great conversation by which their world is being co-created. There is also a reward that may re-enforce resolve, and that is the sheer joy that accompanies all acts of creation. This is what I mean by good conversation as a goad to joy, where I am playing on the title of Schiller's famous poem 'Ode To Joy', as well as making reference to Beethoven's musical rendition in the 'Ninth Symphony'. Insofar as good conversation calls for a creative integration of perspectives, the experience of fashioning what is new and perhaps beautiful has the capacity to inspire all who are involved in the process.

To the extent that bad conversation shies away from this challenge and embraces the opposite, to that extent it becomes not only boring and tedious, but it also remains trapped in the fear of facing its foundations and re-building from there. In the end, what is this kind of conversation but chatter or, in its more current manifestation, 'twitter'?

(iv) Re-valuing versus Devaluing:

AN OBVIOUS QUALITY of bad conversation is the tendency to denigrate or de-value one's opponent. Racism and sexism are some of the sad discursive strategies by which those in vulnerable positions are silenced. Before unjust oppression can take on its more brutal forms, there had to be a corrupt conversation whereby the unity of one group, who would evolve into oppressors, was purchased by the exclusion or devaluation of some other group, who would evolve into the oppressed. The tensions that have been 'resolved' by this strategy are merely driven underground where they fester until they ultimately erupt in some revolutionary outbreak.

Anti-Semitism is currently resurgent, and its function of bringing (false) unity to disaffected groups illustrates the power of a conversation based on scapegoating. Hitler's attribution of treachery to all Jews placed the focus on the theme of betrayal. Yet it is not difficult to see that those who have themselves betrayed their own deepest principles – be they spiritual or secular – avoid thereby their own responsibility by projecting their failure on to the Jews.

One could go on, but the basic point is simple. Speakers devalue others when their own sense of value is threatened and they cannot acknowledge their pain, their fear, or their weakness. Given such a situation, a more viable solution than devaluation is to give positive valuation, to see the good in one's attacker. Of course, this was the approach of Jesus when he counseled turning the other cheek and loving one's enemies. Although I am not a Christian, I can well appreciate the logic of his stance, which does not mean acknowledging the hatred of the de-valuers, but seeking to engage them at the point of their fear and to bestow upon them the value of being worthy partners in discourse.

Now I do not wish to underestimate the difficulty of speaking to those who would devalue others, and fully realize that there might be a point where one must resist the savagery of wrathful individuals who have taken devaluation to the point of destroying their enemies. However, I would also suggest that a discourse devoted to positive valuation of others might forestall or even eliminate such dangerous tendencies. How to do this? A good way to start would be to have honest conversations about one's fears and develop concrete and constructive possibilities for overcoming them. I believe that an authentic sense of value comes from having these kinds of 'courageous' conversations. Doing what is courageous gives one a true sense of value and may prevent the adoption of false value based on the cowardly devaluation of others.

(v) Honesty versus Dishonesty:

MY FINAL POINT ABOUT THE DISTINCTION between good and bad conversations concerns honesty. Socrates was executed by those who were offended by his probing questions about what they thought they knew. Those whom Socrates questioned fell into falsehoods pertaining to their claims to knowledge, but dishonesty in discourse can reach deeper levels in the phenomenon of propaganda. In its political form, propaganda serves the cause of power, where consent to ideological principles is carefully manufactured so that 'stupid' people can be guided to the 'truth' via the guile of clever propagandists. In its economic form, propaganda as advertising serves the cause of mass consumption by manipulating the masses to purchase manufactured goods they might well do without. In short, a public discourse of lies becomes a necessity for the functioning of a complex techno-system.

Yet the price of such 'system-maintenance' is far from cheap. Not only are the lies recognized at some level by the very people to whom they are fed, their widespread proliferation by higher authorities infects the social body by normalizing dishonesty. A possible result is a fatal conflation between truth and lie – fatal because it undermines one's relationship to what is real. When that relationship is so compromised, a kind of mass insanity ensues.

A good conversation, by contrast, neither takes lying for granted, nor considers a commitment to the truth a danger to the social order. Indeed, what would one rather have: living on false foundations that have the appearance of solidity? Or living on the more honest acknowledgment that our foundations are always under construction? If we do not know the absolute truth, we can at least admit with Socrates that we do not know it.

A good conversation, then, must not only seek honesty, but also deal with those who lie from a misguided sense of the good. This means going beyond standing up for the truth as one understands it. It means seeking reconciliation with those who have committed themselves to some kind of lie – perhaps for power, perhaps out of fear, perhaps out of ignorance. Resistance to giving up the lie might be great because it must necessarily cause a profound sense of shame on the part of the erstwhile liar. Nonetheless, the resistance can be overcome as is shown by the reconciliation commissions developed in South Africa in the wake of confronting the suffering engendered by the ideological lie of *apartheid*. Moreover, the process is not a one-sided affair; for just as we must have conversations with those who need forgiveness for their lies, so must we have conversations with ourselves – conversations whereby we confront the shame attendant upon the lies we have told to others as well as to ourselves.

While the pleasures of a discourse based on fanaticism might be great in the short run, the ultimate results are always wretched for its victims, if not for the victimizers as well. Clearly the power of bad conversations is great. They seem to be able to drive out good ones. Yet I can only wonder what could happen if the power of good conversations were properly harnessed – properly harnessed in the sense that the nature of good conversations were clearly understood. One could only find out the answer to this question by having more good conversations and watching how they might drive out the bad ones.

Realizing good conversations

SINCE I AM A TEACHER, my recipe for good conversations is tailored for the classroom where one has to go beyond the one-on-one model of discussion and bring to birth what might be termed a greater discursive space. At the risk of mangling to death a musical metaphor, I would suggest that a teacher functions like the conductor of an orchestra where the students take on the roles of different musical instruments. Since I teach the history of ideas, my musical score is made up of the texts I want them to understand – Plato, Aristotle, Dante, Shakespeare, etc. My goal is to conduct this orchestra in such a way that they, the 'student-instruments', play their own truth as they perform the score.

As one might expect, the tune-up phase is a noisy business, but every conductor must know the power and range of the instruments, and the players must rehearse in a serious way to bring forth melodies that move their hearts and minds. The players in this case are inevitably the audience. However, their friends and all to whom they talk may also get a sense of the music.

How does one begin? After the 'tuning' phase, where the 'student-instrument' spends some time with the score (i.e., reads it on her own and attempts to make some sense of it), the 'conductor-teacher' will ask an individual student to play a 'solo' in response to a question. The solo then becomes the occasion for the conductor to invite another student to play their piece. Should one of the players fumble and produce a discordant note, the teacher might ask them to re-play the piece and, in so doing, encourage him and other potential players to improve their technique. On goes the delicate and subtle interchange between player, conductor, and score – class after class, week after week, month after month – until at last, if all have been working hard, a beautiful harmony begins to be heard. The class mysteriously comes together even if some students have not spoken openly in class. All are engaged. Not only can they grasp the power of the score, they can begin to play in response to each other as the need for a conductor slowly recedes. For I will not always be there, and it is no more the goal of a good teacher to encourage a child-like dependency on the part of the students than it is to silence them on the pretext that they have nothing worth saying. To put it simply, the classroom is an occasion for having good conversations; and when a teacher has managed to realize the discursive potential of her students, then they can take from the class a gift that will serve them well in the wider world and, indeed, make that world a better place.

Having said all this, I do not want to give the impression that the task is an easy one. I might reach the level of embodying a conversation as described above in one out of twenty classes, and that is when I am having a good year! Cynicism about my pedagogical project is thus easy to sustain when one considers how the world is full of fanatics and fools, with whom there is little or no chance of having any kind of meaningful conversation. Some indeed are too far gone with respect to the possibility of having a good conversation and would rather kill than converse. But what should one do? Maintaining silence when one has the privilege of speaking freely seems a betrayal of those who lack such an opportunity. If the world is to change for the better, it can do so via good conversations; and if that must be a slow process, we would all do well to get busy and transform our immediate environments one good conversation at a time. Despite the barriers we have spent generations in building, despite the demands of honesty and courage required to construct the bridges between those who would listen openly and speak honestly, despite all these challenges, I can see no other game worth playing. And if you feel that you are not as honest and courageous as you would like to be, then strive to be as honest and courageous as you can be.

Immodest Proposals For Reform

THE MODERN WORLD MAY BE SAID to have begun with the 'terror' associated with the French Revolution and it may be ending with the terror associated with certain forms Jihadism. The most horrific example of the latter pertains to the events of 9/11 – events that, for many, seemed to suggest the end of the world as we know it. What is or was that world? It may be the world of the 18th-century Enlightenment – a world that lived with the naive faith that a rational discourse would usher in a world of unlimited progress when the irrational forces of aristocratic privilege and religious superstition were quashed. Of course, it did not work out that way; and while one could bring forth many reasons for the failure of Enlightenment hopes, the ignorance of what constitutes good conversations may have played no small role. When one considers that capitalism and communism were both ideological children of the Enlightenment, and that these two siblings could not talk to each other in a meaningful way for the duration of a Cold War that was ever threatening to heat up, one is brought face to face with the failure of public discourse.

What, then, is to be done to teach people to talk to each other when a new form of terrorism threatens to spread a blanket of silence over the world by making us all despair of the possibility of constructive discourse? My answer is a simple one and hopefully not too naive. It is, in essence, to take more time to educate and to discover thereby the joy in co-creative conversation – a joy that far exceeds that of the mindless destruction so dear to the empty heart of the terrorist.

For those who have the luxury of going to university, we, as a culture, seem to think that approximately four years is enough time to educate individuals in either the sciences or the humanities or the social sciences. But if we are to have good conversations – ones where the insights of the sciences can be connected to those of the humanities and social sciences – then the time in university must be doubled and the possibilities for going to university extended to a much greater portion of the population. While one may never reach those who have been drawn into the black hole of ideological fanaticism, one may keep others from being so absorbed by opening to them a discourse where the truths of the spirit and those of the material world are shown to have a multitude of complementary relationships. In other words, one need not choose between the creator and the created, which, to the detriment of discourse, we are implicitly encouraged to do in our current university setting. Therefore, the pioneering of courses emphasizing the big picture, the unity of knowledge, and an interdisciplinary approach to the main problems of our time would all help to make possible a deeper level of conversation. It may still be possible to realize the promise of the Enlightenment by not throwing out the baby of authentic spirituality with the bath-water of fanatical sectarianism.

Beyond the university, but not unconnected with it, is the possibility of establishing a new kind of institution – one that functions as a public forum for an ongoing debate about all questions of relevance to society. It would always be in session, and, with modern communications technology, multitudes could participate. Without the pressure of having to make pressing political decisions, this public forum could get to the depths that should ultimately inform those decisions. While I realize that the devil would be in the details with respect to establishing the rules for such a body, its existence would surely place a value on the role of good conversations while raising to new heights the level of public debate.

An Ending

CAN I BE ABSOLVED OF MY GUILT for all the time I have spent having good conversations with my students and my colleagues while so many have had no such joy? If that joy can be spread to the world by the proliferation of good conversations, my privileges may perhaps be justified and my guilt assuaged.

Ultimately I cannot tell if the good conversations I have had will move beyond the classroom and infuse the fabric of society at large. But I have seen – and I hope my students have seen – what is possible: the co-creation of a world where the political left and right work together in the same kind of harmony that characterizes the left and right hemispheres of the human brain, where means and ends are not sacrificial lambs for each other, where those who have never spoken have found their voice, and those who have never listened have found their ears. I can say that I have heard the harmonies attendant upon deep discourse – faint but unmistakable, sometimes sad but always strangely sweet, bruised by inevitable conflict but always buoyed by a promise of beauty. I have heard this, and my life, such as it is, has been built on the hope that others may also hear this magnificent melody and, on hearing it, make their voices a part of a great symphony that is being composed at the same time that it is played.

Teaching IS

Margo Husby

SPRINGTIME 1987. *I have come to Calgary from my home in British Columbia to visit with family. I am driving west along Glenmore Trail as the late afternoon sunlight bounces off the tall buildings in the downtown core. Further to the northwest, up the hill, is the University of Calgary. It catches my eye and tugs at my heart. I am alone in the car, speaking to the distant campus, "You beat me once when I was young. But I am going to come back and beat you."*

JUNE 2003. I stand on the stage in the Jack Simpson gymnasium as various names are spoken and doctoral hoods are draped over the successful graduates. My name is called and I step forward in my robes of red, blue and gold. Applause, whistles, congratulatory calls echo. My children call out, "Atta go, Mom!!" Someone is ringing a very noisy cowbell. With one hand I clutch my diploma as I raise the other one in a triumphant pumping of air. Under my breath I say, "Gotcha!"

IN 1966, I was a naïve 18-year old, away from the small town and family fishbowl in which I had grown up. Although I managed to avoid serious trouble, I did not manage to attend all classes, complete all assignments or even write all exams. Consequently, the formal letter advising me to seek education elsewhere did not come as a great surprise. I took that advice, married, raised children and, on occasion, took a few university transfer courses at the local college. Twenty years passed before I stepped back on to campus. No longer a naïve teenager, I was now a terrified middle-aged woman determined to achieve my goal but wondering if I really had ability. What helped me discover and believe in myself were my encounters not only with teachers but also with *Teaching* itself. Those encounters led me to doctoral studies in education with a focus on what it means to *be* a university teacher rather than simply *do* university teaching.

This kind of relationship with Teaching is as complex as any other intimate relationship. It has moments of pure joy, of excitement, anticipation, and exhilaration, but it also has moments of pain, depression, doubt, and frustration. That very complexity is what moves Teaching beyond being a job into some*thing*, no . . . into some-*being* more transcendent that invites others into relationship with it.

As I have talked about Teaching having its own ontology rather than being simply a set of rhetorical strategies, educators have definitely raised their eyebrows. But when we start breaking down what makes up this creature we call a 'good teacher', we find very few references to things teachers *did* and more to how they *were* in the world. The universality of the lived experience of the good teacher tells me that Teaching is generative rather than static. It has to be alive in order to achieve its goals. If it were only a set of techniques, it could never be the ever-changing chameleon it has to be. If it were only a series of tasks, anyone could learn to do it. But Teaching is more than the sum of its specific actions in the same way that Friendship is more than the sum of the specific actions of individuals. The reality of Friendship survives despite the ways in which individuals may undermine it. Teaching also endures despite the failures of individual teachers to relate constructively to their students. Teaching calls the teacher to a personal level of fidelity that extends well beyond individual actions. Several examples might help explain.

Teaching and the Teacher

In September 1989, I sat in the first class of a course with a very boring name, General Studies 300. The professor came in, introduced himself and his multiple teaching assistants, and then began to speak about the course. As he spoke, somewhere deep inside myself, I could see a window open. White curtains fluttered in the breeze. Outside the window were springtime green meadows, a shining sun, the bluest of blue skies. A powerful sense of freedom and possibilities filled my being. I remember taking a deep breath, the kind I would take before plunging into a cool lake on a hot summer day. At that moment, I knew I was going to find the vocabulary to express all the ideas, energies, feelings, and questions that had been roiling around inside me for so many years. This was an invitation to growth the like of which I had never before experienced, an invitation I absolutely could not ignore, an invitation that changed my life.

One could say that I met a great teacher; I would agree. But I met more than a great teacher that day. I met a spirit of excitement about ideas and their potential. I met hope, and possibility, and challenge, all of which are intangibles, but all of which were communicated by the professor. These qualities were bigger than he was and he knew it. He invited questioning and interaction and debate because he knew that he was not the source of all the wisdom. We are all in process, all seeking knowledge and understanding. He conveyed the importance of questioning and a warning that those who claim to have found answers can be very dangerous. He invited students to join him on a journey and that is what Teaching does. A teacher can provide information but Teaching itself speaks beyond information. It calls us to do more than regurgitate data on exams and assignments. It calls us to assimilate *what* we know with *how* we go about knowing, with who we are and with how we are in the world.

Flash forward eighteen months. I am in a class on the history of human communication. I submit a five-page paper on Marshall McLuhan and say, "Five pages on him is insufficient; I could write a thesis!" The young professor turns from the film projector he is setting up, looks at me and says, "So write an Honours thesis and I'll be your supervisor." On the surface, this was simply an encouraging statement but it became so much more. Something inside me said, "Remember this moment." And I do, down to the multi-hued winter jackets on the nearby seats, the colour of the professor's shirt, even his ponytail. Those details are irrelevant insofar as understanding material is concerned, but they are the visual echoes of the voice of Teaching that called me to reach beyond the limits I had established for myself. Here I was, a woman in her early forties, who wondered if she had the smarts to get the most basic of degrees, being invited by a professor to do an Honours thesis. Ten short words expanded the universe of possibilities.

I took the offer seriously, did an Honours thesis and, as a result, began to think beyond undergraduate studies. Rounding up all the courage I could muster, I applied for graduate school and was accepted. When I began graduate studies, I was given the opportunity to work as a teaching assistant for the professor who had first inspired me. This is when the voice of Teaching became the loudest. The professor gave all his teaching assistants the opportunity to teach a class and I decided to take advantage of this chance to find out if I could actually teach. I had done amateur theatre, taught Sunday School, led a Brownie pack, run my own ceramics studio with students ranging in age from three to seventy-three, but this was something altogether different. The morning of the lecture, I collected materials and got things set up as the 250 or so students arrived. I clipped on the microphone, turned around, and started to speak. As I did, this current of energy went through my body from head to toe and, as clearly as I have ever heard anything, I heard "**This** is what you were meant to do!" From a religious perspective, one might say that was the voice of God. From a psychological perspective, one might say that was the voice of my ego. Whatever it was, it made a demand on my life; it called me into a new way of being in the university and in the world. It called me into a relationship with Teaching.

Teaching and the Student

OVER THE YEARS MY RELATIONSHIP with Teaching has been rewarding and tumultuous. Teaching reminds me regularly about how frightened I was so that I may continue to empathize with the fear my students feel: be it fear of failure, of not meeting familial goals, of not getting into the programs they want, of not getting the jobs or the futures they want. It reminds me that my own fears have not entirely disappeared. I no longer doubt my intelligence and abilities, but I am only one cog in a huge educational machine, a machine that will roll on without me and, if I fail to pay attention, will roll right over me. If I feel like that as a tenured faculty member, how much more vulnerable must my students be feeling? Because of my own experience, I have a special place in my heart for the non-traditional student, the older student or the international student for whom the university is an entirely foreign country. Sometimes, people who are successful in their professional lives can come back to university with old memories of high school or boring business seminars in their heads. They come with a sense of confidence in their expertise in their jobs and are easily angered when that expertise does not translate into academic confidence. But once they recognize the anger as being grounded in fear and they realize a new way of relating to and communicating material, their countenances brighten, their anger dissipates, and they go on to succeed. I am grateful for the way Teaching uses the fear in my life to help others recognize and overcome fear in their lives.

Teaching also reminds me of the necessity of humility. I make mistakes. I speak flippantly at times and say things for which I need to apologize. Sometimes that apology can be one on one but, all too often, the situation is more like one-on-sixty or one-on-two hundred. As an instructor I no more have all the answers than that professor had so many years ago in my first General Studies 300 class. My students have lived experiences I have not; as a result, they have knowledge and wisdom that I do not. I can learn a great deal from them if I stay open to the many voices of Teaching that blur the various hierarchical boundaries a university has constructed around knowledge. If students and instructors alike enter into relationship with Teaching, then our egos can be more easily set aside so that we may learn from and with each other. I may be an expert on course content, but I am not an expert on how others could or should or might incorporate that knowledge into their lives.

Occasionally, Teaching reminds me to get out of the way and let students learn what they need to learn without me trying to protect them. The first year I taught peer mentoring, a service-learning course, was very difficult. Dr. Tania Smith, the Director of the Curricular Peer Mentoring Network at the University of Calgary, created this course and describes it as follows:

Service learning is a form of experiential education in which a teacher, a community partner and students collaborate in delivering a course that unites the goals of practical service and academic learning. Usually, the community partner is external to the university. However, in the case of peer mentoring, the community partner is the host instructor, the practical service is helping students in that instructor's course improve their learning strategies, and the academic learning for the mentor is in pedagogy." ("Personal Communication," June 29, 2010)

Until then I had an illusion that I had some control over my students' learning environment. This is not the case when students are studying pedagogy with me and then serving as peer mentors in colleagues' classes. When a difficult situation arises as a result of the lack of academic integrity in a student over whom I have no authority, I can feel helpless. All I can do is encourage the ethical and responsible comportment of my students in the midst of a mess. I have to let go of the reins. Teaching reminds me that there is a difference between protecting and smothering, a difference between being present when the bird leaves the nest and doing the flying for it.

Above all, Teaching reminds me of the importance of encouragement. We do not live in a particularly encouraging world. Reality television shows like "Survivor", "The Bachelorette", and "The Amazing Race" celebrate the media version of Social Darwinism. Success is for the conniving, the handsome, the beautiful, the swift, but not for ordinary people who make up most of the world. These shows encourage deceit, relentless competitiveness and the celebration of triumph over others. Their artificiality stands in stark contrast to the needs of the real world and real human relations. This reality demands support and encouragement for others. Encouragement can be as simple as a smile in the hallway, an e-mail to an absent student asking if she is okay, a safe place to cry, a "thank you", or "I like that approach" comments in class. It can be as complex as helping a student dismantle a thesis so her own voice can come through, or as simple as remembering a student's name. Lectures, group discussions and various other things speak to the students' minds; encouragement speaks to their hearts.

The importance of encouragement was made very clear in an email I received a few months after my father's death in 2005. Dad was a high school principal for many years and former students from as far back as 1949 wrote to my mother when they heard of his passing. The following is only one of such messages:

> I am so sorry to hear of your news. In 1963 I was in grade 12, and lost with no idea of what to do with my future. I did not know what a future was as I had grown up in an alcoholic home, with really no guidance whatsoever. Mr. Husby saw potential in me and gave me my first hope by introducing me to a job opportunity after school . . . He told me I had the intelligence to go places, and encouraged me to keep on in school. He did it in an obvious and yet subtle way. He had my teenage respect when I did not even know what that was. A long story shortened, I went on to graduate from [university] with an electrical engineering degree in 1968; started my own company in 1979; joined AA in 1986; raised a family and have 2 granddaughters, and am now a 60 year old . . . living a peaceful contented, serene life. Your dad was the man who gave me hope at the age of 17, and for the longest time, I wanted to thank him. This is my thanks to Mr. Husby; he was a great principal , and a wonderful man who cared.

This man did not speak of subject matter; he spoke of relationship. This relationship is at the very heart of Teaching and it cannot be taught. It must be lived.

While I was working on my dissertation, a friend sent me two quotations she had found in the Bible, quotations that I have taken as my philosophy of teaching and relationship with Teaching:

> The Lord has given me the heart of a teacher that I may sustain the weary with a word. He wakens me morning by morning; he wakens me to hear as those who are taught. (Isaiah 50: 4)

> Not many of you should presume to be teachers, . . . because you know that we who teach will be judged more strictly. (James 3:1)

I must "hear as those who are taught" and I must remember that there are consequences for how I live in relationship with Teaching. The judgment may not be given by any divine power but it will be given by the hearts of the students, students like the one who wrote about my father.

Teaching and the Institution

I MUST ALSO RECOGNIZE that my being as a teacher and my relationship with Teaching as a phenomenological reality are also being judged by departmental and faculty administrators. They receive results from the Universal Student Ratings of Instruction that are completed every year and hear the occasional comment from students who may or may not be enjoying one of my classes. Out of that minimal data, they have to determine my worth in relation to everyone else in the department and faculty in order to assess annual increments. Given that I teach in a research institution and my focus is on my being as a teacher rather than doing research, it comes as no surprise when I am told I need to attend more conferences, present more papers, and get articles published if I want to get greater financial recognition. Presentations and publications are the currency of the academy, especially with the increasing emphasis on creating knowledge and products with corporate marketability. This is simply a fiscal reality, one that research professors recognize and agree to support when they take on research professorships. What space does that leave for those of us who have appointments as instructors rather than professors?

At present an assessment process specifically geared for instructors does not exist at the University of Calgary. Depending upon the department, faculty, or school within the University, an instructor may teach six, eight, or ten courses per year, whereas a research professor may teach four or fewer, depending upon their particular research funding. The competitive nature of the increment process means that the instructor has to come last: researchers rightfully deserve rewards for their tangible production of scientific breakthroughs, articles, conference papers and books. Those of us who do not have research as our primary goal have no discrete measurable items to present with our annual reports. We have contributed to the overall functioning of the university but have not done so alone: every student we teach is also taught by other instructors and professors. At the end of any given year, when I hug dozens of my graduating students at convocation, they are not numbers that validate my individual contribution to the academy. They are people I care about, have become friends with, but that caring and friendship is irrelevant to the institutional processes. We instructors may hold administrative or program co-ordination appointments and serve on committees alongside our professorial colleagues, but we reside in a liminal state, somewhere between the graduate student teaching assistant and the research professor, having greater responsibility than the former and less cachet than the latter.

When I chose the instructor stream rather than the professorial one, I knew there would be a cost and accepted that cost as a reality. I remain content with that choice. The institutional liminality can be frustrating at times, but I was called by Teaching to be a teacher and liminality appears to be part of that vocation. As I live and work as a teacher, my hope is that I share with my students the great gifts of hope, possibility, and encouragement that were given to me during my student years by so many faculty. My M.A. supervisor was willing to take on the challenge of helping me find my voice. Faculty administrators provided support and direction and opened the door for unique teaching and program co-ordination opportunities. The smiles of the wonderful support staff kept me going during difficult days. And I cannot say enough about the sacred souls of the students with whom I have had the pleasure of interacting. Students haven't all liked me; some have felt profound dislike. But they have all taught me something about myself and about my relationship with Teaching. They help me reflect on what is important, on who I am, on who I want to be, and on the great privilege and joy it is to be a teacher.

There was still hope for that girl who failed in 1967, but then put one trembling foot in front of the other in 1988 in order to return to the source of her failure. There is hope for so many more. All I do is introduce them to Teaching and let Teaching invite them into an amazing, life-long friendship.

Learning to Teach

Christine Mason Sutherland

I would wish to be considered as a teacher or as nothing.

WITH THESE WORDS the distinguished scholar Dame Helen Gardner concludes her *Apologia Pro Vita Mea.*[1] Like Dame Helen, whose lectures I attended as an undergraduate, I too would wish to be remembered as a teacher. I look back on over fifty years of teaching in various places and different capacities with a great deal of pleasure – but also with some poignant regrets: I wish I had been able to do more than I have done for more of my students. No doubt many of my deficiencies as a teacher have been caused by my own inadequacy, but I think some of them have arisen from the nature of the university culture, and it this that I want to address, for I believe that some of its current priorities and practices are counter-educational.

I have had a long experience not only of teaching but also of having been taught, and some reflection on those of my teachers who meant most to me may illuminate what has gone wrong, as I see it, with the way so many of us are required to teach in our universities. My first teachers were, of course my parents: my mother, who, I have been told, recited the poetry of Keats to me as she nursed me; my father, who invented stories about the rabbits who lived in the country lanes near our home, and who could spontaneously invent doggerel rhymes and tunes to go with them. He was a great prose stylist, and to the end of his days would correct my writing. Both my parents were musical, father a 'cellist, mother a pianist; and both had exceptionally fine voices, so I learned singing very early. My father taught me part singing before I was three as we walked the dog in the mornings.

I started my formal education at a small village school in rural Norfolk, during the Second World War. My father was in the army, and mother had taken refuge in the rectory of a village so tiny that the whole population could fit into just one of the two large rectory drawing rooms. At the little school in the next village I was given half of a double desk, the other half being occupied by poor Janet, who at eight years old and unable to read, was still in the "babies" class. Whenever she became frustrated, which, understandably, was often, she would "thump" (that was the word these Norfolk children used) thump me across the chest. Retribution came swiftly in those politically incorrect days: the teacher would immediately thump her as she had thumped me. I am not sure that I learnt anything much about reading, writing and arithmetic in that school: what I did learn about was caring. The older children took care of the younger ones, helping them, reassuring them. And I needed reassuring. Strange to say, I was not really afraid of Janet, nor even of "Jerry," i.e., the German enemy, not even when a plane with a swastika on it tried to land in our paddock; but I was afraid of the Head Master, under whose supervision we had to eat our boxed lunches. His name was Mr Huggins, and I was convinced that he was really a bear. It was a little girl called Margery, herself not more than eight years old, who sat with me under the eye of the bear, making sure that he did not suddenly pounce. The sense of community in that school was particularly strong, and in spite of the activities of such as poor Janet, I can remember no bullying at all among these village children.

In May of 1942, my family moved into the city of Norwich, and I was sent to an excellent private school, where I remained for the next twelve years. Good teachers are rare, but I was fortunate enough to meet a few of them during the course of my schooling. And what I chiefly remember about these good teachers was their kindness: they helped me without ever making me feel inadequate to the task of learning, gently explaining what I found hard to understand and never grudging the time they spent with me. On one occasion I was sent back in disgrace to the junior school because I could not do a simple subtraction. I think I was sent back to get a good scolding; but the teacher realized that my problem was fear. So she built my confidence first, and then showed me that I really did know how to do subtractions. Some years later I was having trouble understanding certain features of Latin grammar; again, the teacher responded by building my confidence, telling me that she hadn't understood that particular point until she was in university, and writing out for me a set of helpful notes.

These gifted women not only taught me their subjects – that of course – but taught me too about how to learn and how to be a teacher – how to address not only the mind of the student but her whole personality, including her spirit and her emotions: fear, certainly, but also joy, which is not taught as much as caught from those who have it. One teacher in particular I remember: she lit up the whole subject of English Literature and Language, making it dazzle with possibilities. And it is not only school children who catch joy: time and again I have learned from my university students that it was the passion for the subject that their best instructors taught them: intellectual curiosity and excitement, the sense that there is a whole world of ideas to be explored.

After more than twelve years at my school, I was fortunate enough to be awarded a place at Lady Margaret Hall, Oxford. In the intervening ten months between my acceptance and going up, in what would now be called my gap year, I had my first experience of teaching. I was lucky enough to get a job teaching English Pronunciation at a school in Marseille. My youngest pupil was a little girl of three, my eldest a fine young man of seventeen, scarcely younger than I was myself, at not quite nineteen. It was a school for children with some kind of educational disability – a wide range of problems hardly any of them properly diagnosed. I am not sure that I was able to teach any of them anything very much; but what they taught me was the joy of interaction with enthusiastic young people whose cultural background was very different from mine. For these French children enjoyed life, enjoyed almost everything they did, in spite of their often daunting disabilities. And again I learned the importance of community: every morning began with twenty minutes or so of greeting, kissing each other on both cheeks; and all the men kissed my hand. Furthermore, any quarrels that broke out (and there were many among these flamboyant children) had to be resolved and forgiven with more kissing at frequent intervals – a great time-waster, I thought, in my cold-blooded English way. I realize now that for them relationships with one another and with their teachers were all-important – more important, no doubt, for them, than getting their tongues around the awkward English language I was trying to teach them.

At Oxford, I had the privilege of studying with scholars at the top of their profession who nonetheless gave their primary attention not to research but to teaching. Here I heard superb lectures and became intellectually intoxicated with the excitement of it all. The first lecture I attended – on Shakespeare – was given by a particularly enthralling don, famous, as I later learned, for his abilities as a teacher. I wanted the lecture to go on for ever, so I asked him a question, not knowing that this was against Oxford etiquette. "Haven't you got a tutor?" he growled. But then he repented and tried to reassure me by entering into a discussion of – of all things – the Aeneid! He remembered my first name and my college, and kept sending me messages to visit him and bring my friends – which I did. He became a great inspiration to us all. But exciting as the lectures could be, the heart of Oxford instruction was the tutorial system. Each undergraduate at that time was assigned to a "moral tutor," who not only directed our studies, but also was in charge of us, *in loco parentis*, and could be consulted about anything at all. I was fortunate to be assigned to a great scholar who was also an unusually compassionate and perceptive human being, and she not only taught me herself but also sent me out for tutorials with other dons: for example, I spent one term studying Middle English with the editor of the Oxford English Dictionary.

But I learned not only from my tutors and lecturers but also from other students. Living in college throughout my undergraduate years, I also got to live interdisciplinarity. The women living next to me were studying not English Language and Literature but biology, music, history, medicine – the medic had a real human skull, which we addressed, of course, as Yorick – a whole variety of subjects giving rise to many different insights and approaches which we explored in after dinner coffee parties. Here above all I learned the fascination of discussion and how much we all learn from the exchange of ideas.

And then from learning to teaching:

My next experience was in a tiny school in my native Norfolk. Those of us who wanted to take an after-degree programme in education had first to do a few weeks of teaching practice, and I was fortunate enough to be assigned to a little school in a very small town not far from my home. What I learned there was the importance of character: the headmaster of this junior school gave me a model of what a good teacher should be. I do not know what his scholarly qualifications were. I am reasonably sure that he held no degree from any university. But he understood children, and he made sure that the teachers under his direction understood them too.

At the other end of the scale was my term of teaching practice in London at a highly regarded private school. What I chiefly learned there was how *not* to teach. I was required to sit in on the lessons of the permanent staff, and I remember the agony of hearing a teacher doing violence to *A Midsummer Night's Dream* by picking through it drearily word by slow word, so that the twelve-year-old children could neither hear the poetry nor understand the story. I learned something else of great importance: how to lose or not to lose, one's temper. At this school I taught music as well as English and it was in the music classes – singing classes – that I had my worst problems with discipline. I found that if I pretended to be angry, the students responded very well. But if I really lost my temper they were cowed to such a point that they couldn't sing. It is hard – physically hard – to sing when one is frightened or miserable.

My first experience of teaching as a fully qualified professional was in Canada, in Ottawa, teaching evening classes in high school English. I soon discovered that learning and teaching were quite different enterprises. I had studied *Macbeth* any number of times: it seemed that I had studied it for every important examination for years. But now I had to teach it, and I realized how little I really knew about it. Satisfying the examiners was one thing; helping students to know the joy of it was quite another. So I had quite a lot to learn. Furthermore, I had never before taught mature students. But I found to my delight that they could understand and respond to great works of literature much better than teenagers could. They knew far more about ambition and disappointment and rage and betrayal than most teenagers.

Some years later, this time in a university in the west, I had the frustrating experience of serving as a marker. Knee deep in my own small children, I had no time to teach, but I did keep my mind alive by marking English papers, and in doing so understood for the first time the importance of the intellectual bond between teacher and students. These students were writing their hearts out to an instructor – who was not listening. I felt like an intruder into a very special relationship of which I was not part. I did not attend the lectures and so was not in on the discussion. I could give the students a grade, but I could not contribute to their education.

Back in eastern Canada, in Montreal this time, I undertook preparing students from England for Advanced Level English. This was unlike anything I had done before, much more like the Oxford tutorial than teaching in a classroom. A small group of students came to my house for tutorials twice a week. The problem here was to get them to take a real interest in English literature: they were far more interested in skiing in the mountains. Here I first met the challenge of trying to create intellectual curiosity and excitement in students who were really not interested in study. It was not easy, but in the end we had some good times together nonetheless. But what Montreal chiefly offered me was the opportunity to study at a great Canadian university, McGill. I cannot adequately describe the excitement of being back in a university after fifteen years.

And then back to the west, to Alberta, and again teaching high school English in evening classes. What I especially enjoyed about it was the dedication of the students. If they did not want to be there, there they weren't. They were a very mixed lot in background and intellectual capacity. One student had been a lawyer in his own country and was trying to acquire a better command of the English language so that he could again work in some professional capacity. At the other end of the scale was the elderly cleaning lady who dropped out for a week or two: she was afraid that *Nineteen Eighty-Four* was going to have an unhappy ending, and she didn't want to have to read it. She came back to class when we had moved on to studying another text. Here more than anywhere else I was aware of being of real use to the students. They needed what I had to give them, and were grateful. I met one of them years later, a highly intelligent immigrant woman who had been afraid that her uncertain command of English would keep her out of university: she had just completed a Masters in Social Work.

And so to teaching at a university. I began as a part-time sessional instructor teaching remedial English. Remedial work is tedious, mostly because the students resent having to take it. But even here I learned things about learning and teaching that perhaps I could not have learned anywhere else. All of my students were in my remedial class because they had failed a literacy test; and these were not English-Second-Language students: most of them had attended high school in Canada, but their writing skills were not up to university standards. They therefore came to me after having been told that they could not properly use their own language, and they were humiliated. What my colleagues and I quickly found was that we could get nowhere with such students without giving them confidence. So we tried very hard to find something positive in their writing, something on which we could build; for one cannot build on nothing. It was not always easy. I remember one colleague groaning, "There is NOTHING good about this essay!"

And then there was the challenge and the excitement of helping to form a new Faculty – the Faculty of General Studies, later Communications and Culture – participating in devising the curriculum, creating the courses, engaging in something completely new. My colleagues and I had the opportunity to bring the study of ancient rhetoric into the new curriculum, thus giving academic standing to the teaching of the skills of communication. The heart of the new Faculty was the Heritage course, later split into two. In its first year it was taught almost exclusively by guest lecturers drawn from other Faculties. There were sixteen students and almost as many visiting speakers, many of whom attended all the lectures; and inevitably, discussions and even heated arguments would break out among these academics in a way that must have been bewildering to the students but was exhilarating for the rest of us. Some of the relationships I formed with other visiting lecturers have led to lasting and productive friendships with academics in other disciplines.

The most important lesson I have learned, then, from over seventy years of learning and teaching is the importance of fruitful and trusting relationships – among colleagues, but especially between student and teacher, something that is currently very hard to achieve in our Canadian universities. Some of my colleagues over the years have indeed done so, but they have succeeded in spite of the system, not because of it. The constraints laid upon us by that system make it extremely difficult to provide the context in which a nurturing relationship can be established and true learning on all levels can flourish.

One of the chief problems is that the nurturing and judgemental functions of the instructors are not sufficiently distinguished. Because the instructor, and only the instructor, assigns the grades, she is seen more as judge than as mentor, and there is an emotional disconnect in the relationship. On the one hand she is guide, philosopher and friend; on the other, judge and jury. The trusting relationship between instructor and students is thus compromised from the start. This practice has a further serious consequence: there is an unevenness in the standard between different sections of the same course, it being well known that some instructors mark more stringently than others. Indeed, sometimes students will avoid a section taught by a notoriously hard marker, even if the quality of the teaching is acknowledged to be excellent. In the interests, then, of fairness, as well as in the maintaining of a fruitful relationship between teacher and student, some at least of the evaluation should be done by somebody other than the instructor, ideally a body of examiners. A final examination, carrying a significant percentage of the final grade, and assessed by colleagues in the discipline would remove some of the burden of judgement from the instructor and allow her to be seen as mentor and guide, not as judge and jury. She could work with students, helping them to improve, allowing them to re-think and re-write assignments; and a certain – limited – amount of credit could be given for this willingness to improve – to learn.

Another problem for the relationship between instructor and student arises from overloading: I contend that both students and instructors work far too hard, and that much of this activity is mere busy-work, not productive of real learning, and leaving no time for the leisured reflection and discussion that produce growth. There is a tendency to equate education with the reception of facts: to conflate facts with knowledge and knowledge with wisdom. Facts are of course necessary: we cannot do without them. But facts themselves are inert: they carry no meaning. One of the purposes of education should be to teach students what to do with facts – how to make meanings, and how to understand how meanings are made. This privileging of fact over meaning encourages us to give a lot of little assignments that merely test the reception of facts. The students themselves are often complicit in this process: they prefer a minimal investment in any one assignment. But the upshot is that education is trivialized. We keep digging up our little plants to see if they are growing, with the result that they often do not get to put down firm roots. A related problem is that instructors spend far too much time grading papers rather than educating minds.

Not only are there too many assignments: there is too much assigned reading. Beyond a certain point, the students simply don't do the reading, or if they do, they don't take it in. In our concern to be complete we succeed only in being superficial. It would be far better to assign fewer readings and then to make sure that the students have not only read them but have also understood them. Further readings could be recommended to those who wanted to pursue matters further; even better, we could encourage students to find their own materials. Some of us use this practice in our senior seminars, but it can also be done also at a junior level. This innovation in my own Faculty has been especially fruitful, for in this way we have been able to show students what it means to be a not only a student but also a scholar.

At one level, then, some of the problems in university teaching could be solved without too much difficulty by adjusting teaching practices. But in fact, these troubles are symptoms of a much deeper malaise that is not so easily addressed. Many of them arise from a distorted sense of values. The modern university in the West appears to be driven, like the society in which it is embedded, by the reduction of the idea of prosperity to include only money – ultimate materialism. Scholars are not valued as teachers: they are appointed and promoted according to their success as researchers, and increasingly that research is valued according to how much grant money it brings into the university. Recently the presidents of five major Canadian universities petitioned the government to give more money to research, not because the pursuit of knowledge was a good in itself but because it would make Canada richer. In Britain, matters are even worse: the former Labour government proposed to evaluate research, and therefore research grants, by their "impact," that is, their propensity to make money. In fact, Higher Education now comes within the jurisdiction of Business. But without the tempering influence of the humanities, the arts, and religion, our relationships with one another are in danger of becoming merely exploitative and manipulative: instead of entering into a relationship with other people, we simply use them.

Naturally this culture of materialism affects what the students expect from their university education, what they want to study and how they wish to study it. Some of them come to university with no real intellectual curiosity, no desire to learn, but merely to receive the credentials that will ensure them well-paid positions in the labour force. But most of them, I have found, are dissatisfied with the purely materialistic approach: they are hungry for direction, for some sense that truth and value meet, for some absolutes by which to guide their studies, their careers, their lives. The only lecture of mine that ever drew applause was one in which I had by the exigencies of the curriculum to discuss religion and the reasons for its decline in the Enlightenment. It was not that I was lecturing any better than usual; it was that the students were so eager to hear what I had to say. But unless it is required by the curriculum we cannot give this sense of direction to them. Some of them arrive in their first year with quite strong but relatively unconsidered religious beliefs; and all too often our first step is to take these away from them, to ridicule them or to accuse them of prejudice. Instead we sometimes offer them liberal humanism, itself a kind of substitute for religion, but one without much spiritual force, having ditched its matrix which, like it or not, is Christian theology. Or we may offer them a belief in science, which can, and should, offer no moral guidance, since that is not its job. Alternatively, we can give them valueless postmodernism, urging tolerance without offering any good reason why we should be tolerant of positions so very different from our own.

It is perhaps in this absence of any shared values that we fall back upon materialism: for it is a concern with our material possessions that perhaps comes closest to being a common value. In a secular institution that the modern Canadian university has become, instructors are quite rightly forbidden to proselytize, but also – and I think, quite wrongly – forbidden to admit to or discuss their own fundamental beliefs. Of course, our refusal to teach values comes not only from scientism – which, unlike science itself, has done plenty of damage – but also from fear. Much of the current insistence upon inclusivity is based on the fear that if we offend a certain group of people we shall disturb the peace, and this is by no means an unreasonable fear. But I doubt if our refusal to discuss our values really maintains the peace. It simply drives these issues underground and removes them from the sphere where they might be intelligently and compassionately addressed.

Part of the trouble is no doubt the pattern of argumentation adopted by western societies which envisages such discussion as a form of competition, win or lose. And here traditional rhetoric – the rhetoric of parliaments and law courts – has not served us well. The form of public rhetoric that we have inherited from our traditions, a form that was taught in the Roman period and again in the Renaissance, was *contentio*, a model based on warfare. From it we get such expressions as "The Pen is Mightier than the Sword." The idea that there must be winners and losers, that discussion must take the form of a battle, is not, it seems to me, in this pluralistic age – or indeed, any other – a very helpful model. But there was another form of rhetoric, recognized by Cicero, but not much discussed or theorized, though it was, and is, widely practised. This is *sermo*, the semi-public form of rhetoric, whose model is peaceful social interaction. It is practised, says Cicero, typically at banquets and other social occasions: its oral form is conversation, its written the letter. And what characterizes it is courtesy, consideration – in a word, peacefulness. Its aim is not victory but understanding. And of course it was, and is, practised not just by the public figures and the powerful but also by quite ordinary people, and those we often refer to as the marginalized. But although not exclusively practised by the powerful, it is in itself a potential powerhouse. Some of the key ideas that drove politics and philosophy in the eighteenth century arose from the salons of seventeenth century France. Grass roots discussions contribute to the forming of cultural aspirations which politics must take into account.

Now it appears to me that if as well as teaching the traditional forms of argumentation, where the object is to win, we also taught *sermo*, we might be able to promote that kind of tolerance of other views that we all wish so much to bring about. A start has been made in Rogerian rhetoric, a form of debate in which each speaker is required to demonstrate that she has understood what the previous speaker has said before being allowed to make her own contribution; but we need to take it further. If in the education we offer our students we could encourage them to discuss their very different values and traditions peacefully and charitably, with the aim not to win, but to understand – then we might be able to give them something of real worth to themselves and to the communities in which they will spend their lives.

This is perhaps a counsel of perfection: inasmuch as we fervently believe in our own values and traditions we must want to promote them and to convince others to share them; but if one cannot preach one's beliefs, one can at least live them. As St Francis of Assisi said: "Preach the gospel: if necessary use words," thus suggesting that the most effective proselytizing happens as much by living as by verbal address. One can witness to one's basic convictions without putting them into words. J. S Mill made the same point: he believed, like most earlier thinkers, in the importance of training the will as well as the intellect; but he thought that this would be done less by explicit teaching than by personal influence.

Perhaps, if we live out our beliefs and encourage frank and compassionate discussion among our students we can eventually change this culture of materialism that threatens our societies. Writing in *The Times Literary Supplement* in the spring of 2010, two notable academics, Martha Nussbaum, of the University of Chicago, and Keith Thomas, Fellow of All Souls College, Oxford, have both warned of the crisis in education in both Britain and North America. According to Nussbaum, concentration on purely monetary values and the excision of the arts and humanities from the education of the young threaten not only the democratic form of government but also the very profit-making industries that our leaders apparently want to promote. And Keith Thomas asserts that universities no longer seem to know what they are for: "We cannot determine the purpose of universities without first asking, "What is the purpose of life?"[2] It is to encourage our students to ask that question, and to help them to find some answers to it, however tentative, that we should be directing our efforts.

Endnotes

1. HELEN GARDNER, "Apology Pro Vita Mea," *In Defense of the Imagination*. Cambridge, Mass· Harvard UP, 1982) p 162.

2   KEITH THOMAS. "Commentary," *The Times Literary Supplement*, May 7, 2010, p 15.

Embodied Learning
and Pedagogical Places

Brian Rusted

Throwing myself…

THERE IS A SMALL PILE of poker chips under my feet. They clatter and chatter as I nudge them searching for balance. The chips are at one end of a ballroom in a downtown Chicago hotel. Another pile of chips has been gathered at the opposite end of the ballroom. A rectangle has been meticulously outlined with masking tape on the carpet. The poker chip piles are inside the rectangle while an audience sits at the margins of the long sides, looking into the rectangle. Two performers are standing opposite me just beyond the far end of the rectangle. They are somewhat breathless having just completed a strenuous forty-five-minute performance, a kind of *pas de deux* that claimed the space inside the rectangle and transformed it into a theatre.

Standing inside the rectangle, my task is to discuss the performance scheduled like several thousand other paper or panel sessions being presented at the National Communication Association annual meeting in Chicago in 2009. I had almost a year's notice to prepare a response but still came to the task both advantaged and disadvantaged. The advantage I had over many in the audience was the result of visiting the graduate program at Louisiana State University where the presenters were students. They had organized an experiential workshop that provided an encounter with the creative research methods used to construct this conference presentation. The piles of poker chips were a small reference to the role fate and random probability played in the process: each sentence or gesture was a kind of gamble. The disadvantage I had in responding came from having a script to read prior to the performance.

Performance Studies scholar Dwight Conquergood has characterized *critical* differences between literate and oral forms of knowledge as real, contemporary and fraught with power. For him, these are not benign categories that demarcate stages in communications history or different developmental moments in the human engagement with technology. For Conquergood, they play themselves out in the lives of those who control discourse and those who were marginalized or subjugated by it. He writes that literacy reflects "the dominant way of knowing in the academy", one based in empirical observation and critical analysis . . . anchored in paradigm and secured in print."[1] Conquergood was drawn to "another way of knowing that is grounded in active, intimate, hands-on participation and personal connection."[2] His attention was directed to this knowledge, "anchored in practice . . . that circulates on the ground within a community of memory and practice" because it emerges in and through performance.[3]

Having been disadvantaged by reading the script of this performance, balancing between these knowledges on a mound of poker chips, I recognized this as a reflexive, teachable moment. I could respond easily, critically, analytically to the text that I had read – to the presented words secured by print. Or I could respond to the ephemeral event that had just unfolded for all of us in the ballroom – our sensory encounter with their embodied performance. I could try to interpret the text by mapping it on to various interpretive paradigms, or I could begin by considering how such critical, analytic impulses are the product of a dominant, literate form of knowledge construction, one that professionally I am assumed to espouse and to teach. A counter-narrative to this began with my first university course.

My First University Course:
Education by Wandering About

THE SIXTIES HAD NOT QUITE WORN OUT. I still owed high school some time but I was spending a summer hanging around the university in St. John's. I was wandering along halls and through buildings imagining and anticipating kinds of engagement with what went on there. Things were happening at Memorial that summer. In a chain of art studios on the top floor of the Education Building, Don Wright and David Blackwood were exploring printmaking. Across the campus in the Administration Building's Little Theatre, Michael Cook was directing a summer production of Beckett's *Endgame*, part of a nascent summer theatre festival. I spent mornings in the art studios and afternoons and evenings at the theatre.

Crossing the campus from one building to the other, I would pass a small office full of 16mm film hanging like laundry draped in cloth hampers. Joe Harvey was editing episodes of the television program *Decks Awash*. Produced by the Memorial's Extension Service, it had been a precursor to the National Film Board's Challenge for Change project, inaugurated a year earlier in partnership with Memorial. He edited film sitting at a Steenbeck console. That was his office desk, and he seemed to spend his days like a weaver hunched over a loom shuttling film back and forth, taping some bits together while unceremoniously chopping others and hurling them into bins and baskets. The appeal of this – being able to see both his working and the work – was irresistible. Each time I passed his office, I walked more slowly, lingered longer and eventually made my way out of the hallway and inside. Joe had an assistant, a local actor, musician, and author named Bryan Hennessey. Harvey was generous in sharing his knowledge; the openness of the encounter is surprising even now. He explained how the Steenbeck worked and gave me a first lecture in film aesthetics, demonstrating the effect of splicing different shots together, the consequences of cutting on motion in the frame and so forth. Watching over his shoulder as he shuttled shots on the Steenbeck's platters, I saw that he wove a place. Echoing Conquergood, Andrew Hill has argued that visual culture enters the academy as writing and it is only then that it can be considered a form of knowledge.[4] Although my lingering around Harvey's office does not disprove their observations, it does point to the complex ways that learning and knowledge circulate in the academy.

This was a generative period for cultural work in Newfoundland. Artists like Blackwood or theatre director and radio producer Christopher Brooks were coming back to the island, sharing their education, using it to explore their visions of place. An infrastructure – film, theatre, and visual arts then, and later music and writing – was being established, and most significantly, canonical attention to models imported from elsewhere was giving way to local expressions of place. Harvey's assistant, Bryan Hennessey, worked with his friends to produce music tracks for the NFB's Fogo island films, emulating then popular sounds of electric blues riffs and runs.[5] A decade later, that cohort of musicians would be at the forefront of collecting, adapting and performing traditional Newfoundland music. In less than a decade, Cook would be making tape recordings of vernacular speech to help him write plays set in outport communities. Blackwood came from the places Hennessey and Cook were poised to discover through their art and had already established his vision of how the economics and drama of traditional occupations sustained and constrained body and soul.

Wright, Blackwood, Cook, and Harvey were all employed by the University's Extension Service. Encountering them across the campus that summer was my first University course, what I might call now a directed study, team taught, and experiential. There was no tuition and no grades but those encounters gave me a distinctive set of standards for the classroom, ones that I am still developing and still trying to understand. I was not conscious of being in a classroom, then. What I was learning was not uniformly shared across a roomful of others. What I was learning was not in books, or at least, was not found in books at the outset. Each of these encounters was embodied, immersive, and participatory. I was not simply reading about film editing or theatre directing. My hands were in an acid bath feeling the depth of etching on a copper plate, holding a shot coiled like kelp in the bin next to the Steenbeck, on the ropes hauling curtains, or carrying risers. I could not help experiencing the fullness of these people's lives, the ways work and place and their everyday fit together. Finally, these encounters provided a feeling of *emplacement* in David Howes' sense of extending the experience of embodiment to include or encompass the sensory engagement between body and environment.[6] Walking between buildings, between arts gave me the experience for that summer of being in and knowing a place through them. Being interdisciplinary was of no concern to me then, but the knowledge I came away with is how I understand it now: embodied knowledge, between.

Pedagogy as Restored Behavior

I HAVE TAUGHT MY WAY through at least three different waves of pedagogical discourse: learning styles; inquiry based learning; and community service learning. I call them discourses because they were imposed by the institution to make professors and instructional staff conscious, self-conscious even, about how they set about constructing learning experiences to engage students. There might be a fourth discourse if the need to align teaching with a "research intensive university" is also considered a pedagogical strategy. Living and working through those discourses (all of which the university has textualized and are sedimentary in conversations now about what happens in the classroom), I have tried to maintain my own pedagogical objectives.

A first objective has been to encourage students in having an experience of doing intellectual work. There is so much information available a mouse click away that the experience of thinking is becoming increasingly difficult to achieve in or out of a classroom. Assembly, quotation, description, and file size too often pass as the substance of intellectual work. No amount of summary or précis though can replace the pleasure that comes from seeing an idea in motion, feeling the release of energy when a way of thinking encounters the hurly burly of a subject.

Coming to this experience of intellectual work demands an appreciation of how lives and ideas intersect. Reading theory or scholarly work can appear abstract because no effort has been made to locate it in relation to particular lives or particular times. What impact did travelling voyageur routes by canoe have on ideas the young Harold Innis developed concerning communication and nation? Were there embodied consequences in understanding race and politics for Stuart Hall coming to England from Jamaica? Did Raymond Williams' working class experience in Wales influence his encounters with culture at Cambridge as a student and in the years following World War II working as an adult educator with demobilized military? Answering such questions means appreciating ideas in relation to the times and people that produced them and being better positioned to take them up and adapt them to this place, this time.

Another objective involves putting ideas to work, particularly and especially in relation to personal experience. If intellectual work is going to engage and have vitality, a place has to be made for it in the midst of our lives. The differences made by intellectual work do not happen only on paper. The work of teaching involves encouraging students' fluency with ideas to the point that they occupy a place in their lives. Richard Schechner has often referred to performance as "restored behavior", that is, understanding performance as "recombining bits of previously behaved behavior."[7] Pedagogy shares in this and is itself a performance practice that endeavors to have performers and audience alike restore life to ideas, recombining them in the midst of their own experience.

My Second University Course:
Teaching through Performance

A DECADE OR MORE after my first university course, I am back in Newfoundland recreating the intellectual world of English literature for summer session students at Memorial's temporary campus in Grand Falls. The paper mill was still in operation then, with world demand for newsprint fueling the employment cycle of logging, pulping and paper making. Local life was permeated by the economy's acrid scent. The majority of students were already teachers and were spending part of their summers upgrading credentials with the kind of inter-session courses I had been asked to teach: introduction to poetry, introduction to drama, introduction to 20th century British fiction and so forth.

There were a number of constraints on teaching these classes, not ones I had anticipated or been given advice on. In the drama classes, students were happy to read scenes aloud prior to discussing them but if I was fortunate enough to have access to a film version of a play to screen, those raised or working in the Pentecostal school division excused themselves and waited respectfully in the hall until the film was finished. Allusions found in modern poetry or intertextual references in novels would not resonate with the students. There were no bookstores and beyond prescribed books from their own school years, they had little to read. To teach a play like *Endgame*, I needed to perform the history of modernism for Beckett's creative choices to make sense to the class. Although I came to appreciate the labor involved in making such an intellectual and cultural world present for my students, I did not succumb to missionary zeal. The learning process began with unraveling my middle class expectations acquired in the otherworldly St. John's. The encounter – one of my most important teaching and learning experiences – made me think long and hard about how to teach the literary and interpretive skills these genres asked of students. Why train them to be sophisticated consumers of cultural products they did not have access to?

If this was a dilemma that required a solution, it presented itself accidentally and produced what I see now as my first class in performance studies. A large tent had been standing for most of the summer where the secondary road coming around the southern end of Exploits Bay met the Trans-Canada highway. Some students were familiar with it and knew it was the base of an itinerant, evangelical ministry that held revival meetings there on weekends. Rather than apply the interpretive skills we had developed in relation to canonical texts from our prescribed reading list, I encouraged those who were interested to use them on aspects of their lives such as this. For those who took up the challenge, the results were exciting: their intellectual and critical skills helped them develop analyses of the tent meetings, its props, dramatic monologues, plots of healing, the ways boundaries and social exclusions were created through appeals to faith and the threat of evil. They learned something about the place of performance in their everyday lives, but this alone was not transformative. Their integration of critical practices with their experience of place revealed the pleasures and relevance of doing intellectual work. Theory and method and criticism were no longer directed towards the appreciation of literary texts that stoked a sense of social marginality. These intellectual skills became habits of mind, taken up in their embodied and emplaced experience.

...To the Wolves:
Rediscovering Pedagogical Places[8]

SARAH PINK HAS SUGGESTED that ethnographers create "ethnographic places." These are not the places where research and fieldwork occur; they are constructions of places ethnographers craft in representing and communicating their research.[9] A classroom is a variety of such ethnographic places, a pedagogical place. It is not (frequently) where ideas come from; it is not (frequently) where a teacher first encounters research that forms a curriculum. As a pedagogical place, a classroom is a shared fiction produced by the engagement that students and teachers alike have with ideas, with research, and with their sense of engagement with the social world.

Most discourses about teaching and learning seem to begin in or start from this pedagogical place. The process of teaching is initiated by the teacher and moves outward or at least anticipates, predicts or prescribes a movement outward into the lives of the students. In articulating "critical performance pedagogy," Elyse Lamm Pineau suggests that one dimension of this teaching practice "puts bodies into action in the classroom because it believes this is the surest way to help those bodies become active in the social sphere."[10] She traces the foundation of this pedagogy back through Giroux, Friere to Dewey and Marx, noting the responsibility of public educators to critique rather than indoctrinate through a reflexive negotiation of power inside and outside the classroom.

At the heart of this is the effort to return the body to the classroom. As Lamm says, students and teachers effectively have been schooled to forget "their" bodies when they enter the classroom in order that they might give themselves more fully to the life of the mind."[11] Or in the blunt image from Tami Spry, "for me, academe has always been about speaking from a disembodied head."[12] Returning the body to the classroom is an acknowledgement that students live in their bodies, know through their bodies, and that teaching and learning or being in a pedagogical place require them "to struggle bodily with the course content"[13] because "an active body *learns* in ways that are eminently more personal, applicable, critical, and long-lasting than any other teaching method."[14]

Pedagogical places are not solely about the negotiated emplacement of teacher and student, any more than they are just about the liberatory ideas that teachers imagine students will carry actively into their social lives. The borderlands of pedagogical places though should not be seen as lying at the edges of classrooms or the beginnings and endings of courses, nor do they originate in an antecedent place of books and theory. Pedagogical places encompass the sensory and relational experience of the institution, the department, or the program that permits certain kinds of things to happen and not others, that fosters and supports certain pedagogical practices and not others, that sustains a community of learning beyond the paradigm of the isolated teacher in a disembodied class. Increasingly, performance is being aligned with other forms of creative research and creative pedagogies.[15] For such embodied pedagogies to have a place in the academy, to provide students opportunities to inhabit theory and research bodily, it is important to recognize these practices as extensions beyond the classroom. They extend beyond being classroom strategies. They extend beyond the reinforcement of multiple classrooms that may share the same sensibility. They extend pedagogy into the between spaces of institutions, not just outward into the imagined lives of the students.

The proverbial phrase, "thrown to the wolves" comes from Aesop's fable about "the old nurse and the wolves," a threat made to silence a child. A wolf overhears the nurse, takes her performative speech literally and then gets frustrated waiting for the child to be thrown. The title of Brisini and Waychoff's performance, "Throwing Myselves to the Wolf" puns on this phrase connecting it with a postmodern troubling of unified subjectivity. Their script is densely citational to the point that a reader begins to wonder what such a complex, intertextual piece has to do with the threat of silence. The script frustrates those expecting the performative use of language and yet it is likewise silent about the bodies of the performers. Minimal instructions accompany some lines ("jump/squat"; "turn out in opposite directions" etc.), while a whole scene called "Postures," described as taking fourteen minutes to perform provides no directions at all.

Brisini and Waychoff's embodied knowledge is not fixed by text or discourse; it emerges in performance, torquing the words in ways that print does not convey. If the audience catches allusions, they feel the words do different things than in a more familiar print context. Bringing their bodies into play in the performance of theory evokes and restores the pedagogical place that enabled their presentation, other students, other professors that sustain, participate in, or critique such embodied engagement with research. What is called for in the Chicago hotel ballroom is not an interpretation of the meaning of their text or an evaluation of the creative methods they have deployed to produce it. What is called for is what their performance calls forth: the creative between of students and faculty emplaced by transformative, pedagogical practices.

Endnotes

1 Dwight Conquergood. "Performance Studies: Interventions and Radical Research." *The Drama Review* 46:2 (2002), 146.

2 Ibid. 146

3 Ibid, 146.

4 Andrew Hill. "Writing the Visual." Milton Keynes: CRESC Working Papers Series No.51 (2008), 5.

5 Bryan Hennessey. "Working in a Fledgling Film Industry," *Newfoundland Quarterly* 99:4(2007), 22-5.

6 See Sarah Pink's discussion of Howes in *Doing Sensory Ethnography*. (London: Sage, 2009), 25.

7 Richard Schechner. *Performance Studies: An Introduction.* (London: Routledge 2002), 28.

8 The performance piece in Chicago that I was responding to was Travis Brisini and Bryanne Waychoff's "Throwing Myselves to the Wolf" presented as part of the Performance Studies Division's program at the National Communication Association's annual meeting.

9 Pink, *Doing Sensory*, 42.

10 Elyse Lamm Pineau. "Critical Performance Pedagogy: Fleshing out the politics of liberatory education." *Teaching Performance Studies*. Nathan Stucky and Cynthia Wimmer, eds. (Carbondale, Illinois: Southern Illinois University Press 2002), 53.

11 Pineau, "Critical Performance Pedagogy," 45.

12 Tami Spry. "Performing autoethnography: An embodied methodological praxis." *Qualitative Inquiry* 7:6 (2002), 715.

13 Pineau, "Critical Performance Pedagogy," 50.

14 Ibid, 52.

15 See for instance, Patricia Leavy. Method Meets Art: Arts-Based Research Practice. (Guilford Pres, 2008), or Catherine Camden-Pratt. "Social Ecology and Creative Pedagogy: using creative arts and critical thinking in co-creating and sustaining ecological learning webs in university pedagogies."

Transnational Curriculum Inquiry 5:1 (2008), 4-16. Retrieved from http://nitinat.library.ubc.ca/ojs/index.php/tci

THE STUDENT

Millennial Angst
Students, Universities, and Change

Jo-Anne André

O VER THE PAST DECADE, universities across Canada have been busy transforming themselves, adding so-called "digital libraries" open 24/7, converting more space to meeting rooms for student groups, developing new "student success" centres, tailoring new orientation programs for students *and* their parents, and adding shiny new food courts and residence buildings. Of course, some of the new infrastructure replaces aging buildings that would cost more to fix than to knock down and replace. But driving many of the physical transformations is an unprecedented emphasis on student engagement and satisfaction, one that compels universities to put ever more effort and resources into catering to the new student demographic – the *Millennials*.

Who exactly are the Millennial generation? Why and how are universities changing to meet their expectations? What are the implications for professors called upon to teach this new generation of students? And how can universities manage change intelligently, avoiding the many potential pitfalls that line the road ahead?

The Millennials

MUCH OF THE PICTURE of Millennial generation (also known as *Gen Y* or the *Net Generation*) derives from the work of Neil Howe and William Strauss, authors of *Millennials Rising* and

Millennials Go to College (2003). They define the Millennials as the generation born in 1982 and after, a wave of students that has been hitting the shores of post-secondary education each year since 2000. Howe and Strauss describe the Millennials as *special, sheltered, confident, team-oriented, conventional, pressured,* and *achieving,* seven core traits, they say, that characterize this new breed of student. They explain that, compared to the students who preceded them, the Millennials "are more numerous, more affluent, better educated, and more ethnically diverse. . . [with] a new focus on teamwork, achievement, modesty, and good conduct" (2003, 14). And, of course, there is this generation's deep familiarity with technology, making them what Marc Prensky (2001) calls "digital natives."

A generation of youth who have grown up protected and lavished with parental attention and resources, the Millennials possess the sense that they are "special." According to Howe and Strauss, they are close to their parents, and their parents tend to be so-called "helicopter parents," hovering over and involved in their young adult children's lives and education even well into their university years. Howe and Strauss describe the Millennials as much more team-oriented than the Generation X students that preceded them. In part, their team orientation comes out in their obsession with social contact, addiction to texting, and nearly constant use of social networking media such as Facebook. Howe and Strauss (2003) also note that this new generation of university students are conventional, feel pressured to succeed, and tend to be heavily focused on structured activities, studying, grades, and achievement.

Demographically, the Millennial generation is a large one; numbering 80 million in the U.S. alone, this generation is about 30% larger than the Baby Boomer generation (Howe & Strauss, 2003). In Canada, this increase is reflected in the rise in university enrollment, which grew 38% over the nine years from 1997/98 to 2006/07 (CAUT, 2010). The majority of post-secondary students today are female, with women accounting for 58% of undergraduate students in Canada today (CAUT, 2010). Not surprisingly, university students tend to come from higher income families. According to CAUT, the Canadian Association of University Teachers, "in 2006, youth aged 18-24 with parents earning more than $100 000 . . . were almost twice as likely (49%) to have been enrolled in university than those [with] parents earning less than $25 000 (28%)" (2010, "Students," 1). A substantial number of university students today also work part-time. Economist Christine Neill explains,

> Many more undergraduate students work part-time today than did 20 years ago (when a third of students worked). . . .
>
> [A]bout 39 percent of male and 49 per cent of female full-time students in Ontario work during the academic year. Just over 15 percent . . . work 20 or more hours a week; six to seven percent work more than 30 hours [a week]. (Cited in Kershaw, 2009, "Is it a win-win?" para. 4-5)

Later in this chapter, we'll look more closely at the Millennial generation and at the expectations they bring with them into university classrooms, but first let's look at the bigger picture: why and how are universities changing to meet this group's expectations?

University Responses to the Millenials

IN AN EARLIER ERA, the arrival of a new generation of students at post-secondary institutions would have had little impact on the ways in which those institutions organized themselves and set their priorities. Students would have had no choice but to adapt and thrive, struggle silently, or give up and leave. University admission was, after all, a hard won privilege to be thankful for. Students had modest expectations, and student engagement was something students had to find for themselves – not something that university administrators obsessed over in the backrooms of academe. (And "Nessie" was just a mythical sea creature in some Scottish lake.)

Today, though, universities find themselves in a much more competitive environment as they struggle to compete with other post-secondary institutions for students. Older, well established universities find themselves competing with colleges newly re-minted as universities. In British Columbia and Alberta alone, seven post-secondary institutions have been granted university status since 2008. Recently, this increasingly competitive educational marketplace has combined with economic forces to produce less stable and predictable government funding for universities, returns on investments, and student enrollments. All in all, it's not a great time to be running a university.

The post-secondary landscape has changed in other ways as well. With provincial governments implementing Key Performance Indicators tying performance to funding and with the advent of university evaluation and ranking tools like *Mclean's* magazine's annual ranking of universities, CTVglobemedia's *Globecampus* website for "comparing, and ranking schools," and the *National Survey of Student Engagement*

(NSSE, pronounced "nessie"), universities face new pressures to be accountable and to compare favourably with their peer groups in order to maintain their funding and to attract potential students. Oddly, universities have added to this competitive environment by creating a new association of Canadian universities – the *G-13* – to benchmark themselves against using their preferred criteria ("Group of Thirteen," 2009). Alas, whether these competitive ranking systems are genuine forces for improvement or insane zero-sum games in which, ultimately, everyone loses as universities spend an ever-increasing proportion of their funds on glossy publications and public relations campaigns is a question well worth asking, but one that I don't have room to explore further here. The bottom line is that, for better or worse, universities have become participants in an increasingly competitive environment in which they have to do – or to appear to be doing – everything they can to meet governments' KPI targets and students' wishes and expectations.

The Millennial generation has arrived on Canadian campuses just in time to reap the rewards of the increasingly fierce competition among universities. The generation that has been described as "special" and "sheltered" now expect a post-secondary experience tailored to meet their needs and expectations. And those expectations are not trivial. As Howe and Strauss (2003) explain,

> Millennials (and their parents) can be very demanding. They (and their parents) tend to be fixated on having only the "best" of this or that. They (and their parents) place enormous emphasis on the quality of campus life – from the strength of school spirit to the safety of dorms to the quality of mental health services and mentoring programs. (65).

Somewhat ominously, Howe and Strauss also note that, given the demanding nature of prospective university students (and their parents), "their list of 'needs' could bankrupt even the wealthiest of universities" (65).

Perhaps not surprisingly, in response to the increasingly competitive environment and to the arrival of the Millennials on campus, universities appear to be devoting a larger amount of resources toward student services relative to expenditures on instruction. According to the *Trends in College Spending 1998-2008* report issued by the Delta Cost Project, which compared over 2000 U.S. colleges and universities, on average, the 152 universities in the *public research* category increased their expenditures on instruction by 10.1% over the previous 10 years, compared to an increase of 20.1% on student services, 19.9% on administration ("institutional support"), and 26% on operations and maintenance (Desrochers, Lenihan, & Wellman, 2010). The authors of the report noted that "in all sectors, the instruction share of spending was lower in 2008 than both five and ten years prior"; public institutions, they noted, "have shifted resources into increased spending on administration, with comparable shifts to student services in public research institutions" (22).

In Canada, information drawn from the *CAUT Almanac of Post-Secondary Education 2009-2010* suggests similar trends. The authors note that "over the past 30 years, spending on academic salaries as a proportion of total university expenditures has declined steadily," from 32% of total expenditures in 1977 to 20% in 2007 (CAUT, "Finance," 1). At the University of Calgary, the patterns of expenditure confirm a relative growth in expenditures on the student services side. From 2006 to 2009, for example, the number of management and professional staff in Student and Enrolment Services increased 39.5%, compared to an increase of 18.5% for the same job category in faculties (University of Calgary OIA, 2010b). The shift is even more evident in other ways, as the University of Calgary attempts to do everything it can (short of tuition reductions) to cater to the needs and expectations of the Millennial generation. Millions for the Students' Union to dole out in grants to improve services and spaces for students on campus each year? *Check*. Leather chairs and spacious study and lounge areas? *Check*. Development of a new digital library and "student success" centre? *Check*. Abolition of an annoying university writing requirement? *Check*.

Implications for Professors

MILLENNIAL STUDENTS have brought a new set of expectations with them into university classrooms and, along with those, a new constellation of opportunities and challenges for their professors. In particular, professors must deal with a new focus on grades and attitude of entitlement among students; accommodate students' preferences for group work, while guarding against plagiarism; find new ways to handle sensitive topics in the classroom; embrace technology and find a balance among instructional approaches; and build on the positive attributes of Millennial students while developing their research skills. These are considerable challenges and ones that will no doubt evolve over the next decade as new information and communication technologies emerge and as universities continue to transform themselves to attract and engage the coming waves of Millennial students.

1. Dealing with a new focus on grades and attitude of entitlement

ACCORDING TO HOWE AND STRAUSS (2003), Millennial students expect good grades and are more apt than previous generations of students to complain about "unfair" grades (83), a trend that just about any professor on any campus these days would attest to. A study by Greenberger, Lessard, Chen, and Farruggia (2008) appears to confirm what professors have increasingly been noticing since the arrival of the Millennial generation on campus. In that study, 66% of the 466 students who responded to a survey on "academic entitlement" felt that if they told their professors that they had been "trying hard," their professors should consider their effort in determining their course grades (1196). In the same study, just over 40% of students agreed with the statement "If I have completed most of the reading for a class, I deserve a B in that course," and 34% agreed with the statement "If I have attended most classes for a course, I deserve at least a grade of B" (1196). Greenberger et al. found that students who had a greater sense of academic entitlement indicated that their parents expect them to outshine others in their academic performance and provide them with material rewards when they do well. These students also experience more anxiety about their grades, and . . . have an extrinsic orientation toward their coursework that emphasizes getting good grades over the pleasures of learning and mastery. (1201)

Greenberger and her colleagues speculate that attitudes of academic entitlement may be encouraged by several factors, including anonymous course evaluations, trends toward grade inflation, and the widespread use of e-mail, which allows students greater access to their professors and reduces status distinctions between students and their professors. Others point to students' experiences in K-12 and their propensity to "confuse the level of effort with the quality of work" (Roosevelt, 2009, 1).

Faced with this new focus on grades and attitude of academic entitlement, what are professors to do? They might consider redesigning their courses to meet Millennial students' desire for more structure, frequent feedback, and more small projects rather than heavily weighted (and anxiety-producing) tests and large projects (Howe & Strauss, 2003). To encourage realistic expectations about grades, they should take care to outline their grading practices, share their marking rubrics with students, and provide examples and descriptions of what constitutes A-, B-, and C-level work. And, of course, professors may need to remind students that grade appeals sometimes result in *lower* grades. Above all, professors should be fair when grading and not give in to students' demands for special treatment. As Greenberger and her colleagues (2008) point out, "If students learn that they can get a high grade with minimal effort, or that trivial excuses often result in special favors . . . we should not be surprised if they develop entitled attitudes" (1202).

2. Accommodating students' preferences for group work — while guarding against plagiarism

HAVING BEEN SOCIALIZED in high school to an emphasis on group projects and collaborative learning, students in the Millennial generation are team-oriented and typically prefer working in groups rather than independently (Howe & Strauss, 2003). They also tend to prefer learning by doing (experiential learning) and appreciate learning for a practical purpose (McNeely, 2005). In the classroom, Millennials' preference for group work is good news for professors, who can use team projects to motivate and challenge students and to reap the advantages of collaborative learning while lightening their marking loads in the process. Nonetheless, for professors who cling to the view that grades should reflect only *individual* effort and achievement, the shift to more group projects and group grades may not be an entirely comfortable one.

In some cases, assignments may combine both individual and group components. Howe and Strauss (2003) suggest having students "perform independent assignments in a framework that requires them, at some final stage, to integrate all the work into some collaborative output" (p102-103). This is an approach that I use in my *Rhetorical Communication* course: early in the term, students form groups around controversial topics, write individual papers analyzing persuasive texts in the debate, and collaborate on a group presentation providing background on the controversy and bringing the individual presentations into a cohesive whole. When it comes to peer critique, however, Howe and Strauss (2003) warn that "having students debate or critique each other's work (an approach that typically energized Boomer students) is a difficult challenge that often misfires among Millennials, especially when staged before an entire class" (102).

As they rethink their courses and craft assignments for this new generation of students, professors must keep in mind that this generation's predilection for collaborative work has its dark side: increased rates of academic misconduct. In a U.S. study by Greenberger et al. (2008), just over 60% of undergraduate students said that they had collaborated on "what was supposed to be an individual assignment, 52% of students admitted to cheating on a test, 51% said that they had submitted work copied from other students' work, and 47% said that they had helped someone else cheat on a test (1200). A large-scale study by Christensen Hughes and McCabe (2006) on academic misconduct in Canadian post-secondary institutions reported slightly lower numbers, with 53% of undergraduate students and 35% of graduate students admitting to cheating on written work, and 18% of undergraduate students and 9% of graduate students saying that they had cheated on a test. Participants in this study included nearly 15 000 undergraduate students and just over 1 300 graduate students in ten universities and one degree-granting college in Canada.

It is clear, from the Christensen Hughes and McCabe study and from other research, that students' perceptions of what constitutes cheating differ somewhat from what their instructors consider cheating. A recent article in the *Globe and Mail* reported that "80 per cent of high school students rated collaborating on an assignment despite a teacher's instructions as only a minor infraction, compared to 27 per cent of faculty" (Hammer, 2010, A4). It seems that these differing perceptions have roots in aspects of culture. In interpreting their findings, Christensen Hughes and McCabe (2006) comment that their results "may represent a clash between an emerging collaborative student culture and a more traditional, individualistic faculty culture" (15). They go on to write, "Many students have arguably come to realize that working collaboratively can be time-efficient and learning-effective, and can lead to higher grades for everyone involved" (15). Sowden (2005) adds another dimension to this picture of Millennial students, noting that students from other cultures may bring with them ideas about "the communal ownership of knowledge" and cultural norms that encourage students to value group consensus and "sharing knowledge and responsibility" over western values in which "individual effort and self-reliance are considered meritorious, and mutual assistance is not encouraged outside strict boundaries" (p226-227). Furthermore, as Howe and Strauss (2003) observe, today's youth pop culture offers an array of mash-ups and remakes "that efface the identity of the author" and embody "imitation, simulation, and condensation" with less focus on "the personal, the authentic, and the original" (119-120). In such a milieu, they say, young people "may see nothing wrong with simply rearranging, in a report or paper, a thought that someone else has expressed with considerable elegance" (120).

In an era in which unsanctioned collaboration, plagiarism, and other kinds of academic misconduct appear to be on the rise, professors need to be vigilant about the academic integrity of student work. But, more importantly, they should consider taking a proactive approach to dealing with these problems. Christensen Hughes and McCabe (2006) suggest that "Given a student culture that values collaboration, faculty should be realistic when assigning independent work and be clear about their rationale for doing so" (15). Professors should also clarify their expectations about what constitutes unacceptable collaboration and use of sources, and they should make an effort to teach students about proper citation practice and documentation styles and not assume that students (particularly students from other cultures) are familiar with North American norms of academic citation (Sowden, 2005). When designing assignments, professors should generally modify their assignments each year and attempt to develop creative assignments that are unique to the class or that must be done in a sequence of smaller graded tasks and presentations, thereby discouraging students from buying prewritten papers from online essay mills. Professors might also consider adopting more group assignments as a constructive way of channeling students' preferences for collaboration.

3. Handling sensitive topics in the classroom

WITH MILLENNIALS POPULATING today's classrooms, new challenges may arise related to course content and in-class discussion. While the current generation of students are less likely than their predecessors to engage in debate in class (Howe & Strauss, 2003), professors, particularly those in humanities and social sciences, may find it increasingly tricky to teach about issues with ethical dimensions. Howe and Strauss (2003) predicted that professors "could start hearing complaints from parents who differ with their points of view, especially if their collegiate children report back home that they are getting more attitude and opinion than knowledge in the classroom" (2003, 84). To take just one example, students from this ethnically diverse generation may resist being taught that racism is prevalent in society when their personal experience interacting with a diverse student population seems to indicate that the opposite is true. As Howe and Strauss (2003) remark, "the old association between minority race and social disadvantage" may be eroded in Millennials' eyes by "the rapidly rising number of affluent nonwhite households" and "the high visibility of numerous very wealthy nonwhite athletes and other celebrities" (96). Howe and Strauss offer the following advice to faculty members from the Boomer generation:

> Faculty would do well to remember that the various causes of the 1960s . . . are as chronologically distant from today's Millennials as World War I and Prohibition were to Boomers when they were in college. Faculty who envision Millennials as instruments for completing their "half-finished" societal agendas may come away disappointed, frustrated, and

deeply critical of these new youth for the "lessons" they have supposedly "forgotten." (2003, 104)

In short, the generation gap in the classroom may become especially problematic in courses dealing with issues of race and gender.

In such an environment, professors should take care to emphasize the published research underlying their in-class assertions about racism or sexism. Even more constructively, they should take advantage of Millennial students' preference for experiential and inquiry-based learning. For example, they could design research projects through which students might learn first-hand through interviews with minority group members about their experiences with racism. More simply, they could have students analyze primary sources in class for evidence of racism, sexism, or other kinds of bias. Undergraduate student Carie Windham recounts how one of her instructors successfully managed to use her students' preferences for learning through first-hand exploration:

> Rather than discussing bias . . . journalism professor once asked my class to analyze several articles and discuss their diction. We arrived at the conclusion that the authors' bias was implicit in their work with little direction. We left class that day with both a sense of accomplishment and a deeper understanding of the journalistic themes the professor had hoped to explore. (2005, 58)

Professors should keep in mind that while Millennials may reject identity politics, they are a socially engaged generation of students who want to be active in political, social, and environmental causes; interested in making their world a better place, they may well embrace issues from global warming to disparity in income distribution (Howe & Strauss, 2003). To engage this generation of students, professors should consider how they might take advantage of students' preference for learning by doing and how they might integrate so-called "community service learning" elements into their assignments.

4. Embracing technology and finding a balance among instructional approaches

A DISCUSSION OF UNIVERSITY STUDENTS today would not be complete without a closer look at the ways in which technology has shaped this generation's learning styles, ways of thinking, and classroom expectations. Marc Prensky, who has dubbed this new generation "digital natives" (as opposed to their "digital immigrant" instructors), estimates that today's students have typically spent "over 10 000 hours playing video games," double the number of hours they've spent reading (2001, 1). Other research points to this generation's propensity to use social networking websites like Facebook. In their study of 596 first-year students at five British universities, Jones and Ramanau (2009) found that over 95% of students aged 25 and under had used social networking websites, compared to just over 20% of their cohorts aged 35-and-up and that nearly 82% of the younger group of students used social networking sites on a daily basis. Prensky (2001) argues that, as a result of their immersion in a digital environment their entire lives, today's students not only use technology differently but "*think and process information fundamentally differently* from their predecessors" (1). He goes on to explain that this generation "function best when networked. They thrive on instant gratification and frequent rewards. They prefer games to 'serious work'" (2).

When it comes to the classroom, then, what exactly do Millenials want? Prensky (2001) argues that today's students "have little patience for lectures, step-by-step logic, and 'tell-test' instruction" (3). In a case study using focus groups of twenty-six students and five professors at one small California university, Forkum (2008) found that while professors tended to prefer lecture format for instruction with occasional use of PowerPoint, their students were unhappy with that delivery method and preferred instruction that integrated "more technology and software, along with collaborative learning experiences" (2008, 76). Students indicated a preference toward the use of blended learning as well as multi-media, with, as one participant put it, "animation or images that relate to the knowledge they want us to learn" (77). Students in Forkum's study also warned against overuse of PowerPoint and expressed "frustration and dissatisfaction with the lack of technology awareness by the faculty" (80). Forkum concluded that the Millennials "are demanding their courses have the appropriate content delivered in state-of-the-art technology, using appropriate software, and cooperative learning" (87). More large-scale studies report similar findings and unequivocally indicate that the Millennial generation of students expect technology to be used in their courses. In a 2004 survey of students at thirteen U.S. universities, 41.2% of the 4374 participants (of whom 95% were twenty-five years old or younger) expressed a preference for classes with *moderate* IT (information technology) use, while 30.8% indicated that they preferred classes with *extensive* IT. Less than 26% of students said they preferred classes with *limited* or no IT use. Perhaps not surprisingly, the results varied by discipline, with preference for extensive use of IT in courses highest among engineering and business students. Across all disciplines, Fine Arts students were most likely to indicate a preference for courses with no technology (9% of responses). (Forkum, 2008.)

Perhaps the most radical response to the Millennials' preferences for technology in learning would be the game-based-learning approach advocated by Prensky (2001). Based on the idea that "students learn better when they are having fun and are engaged in the learning process" (Spectre & Prensky, n.d., 1), educational software promotes "accelerated, effective learning" through "questions, mistakes, and multiple senses; feedback and reinforcement; challenge, involvement and relevance; and 'doing,' through simulation and cognitive apprenticeship" (2). Prensky cites the example of *The Monkey Wrench Conspiracy*, a game used around the world to teach engineering students to use CAD software. In the game, developed by his company in collaboration with engineering professors, the student user "becomes an intergalactic secret agent who has to save a space station from an attack by the evil Dr. Monkey Wrench"; to do so, "the learner must employ CAD software] to build tools, fix weapons, and defeat booby traps" (Prensky, 2001, 5).

Of course, most of today's university classrooms are a far cry from what Prensky might imagine as the ideal digital environment to optimize learning for the Millennial generation. Typically, the response among universities to the arrival of the "digital natives" has been to promote widespread use of blended learning, in which face-to-face classes are combined with online learning materials, forums for discussion, and other learning activities supported on a course management system like WebCT, Moodle.com, or Blackboard. Research seems to support the benefits of blended learning. In a study evaluating blended learning combined with a concomitant 50% reduction in face-to-face class time in a course on American government, Pollock and Wilson (2002) found that students in the blended learning course, which incorporated online learning modules, outperformed their peers in a traditional classroom setting on an objective pre- / post-test of knowledge gains. Nearly three times as many of the students in the blended learning class showed gains of four points or better. In addition, students in the blended learning class rated the course more favorably "in the helpfulness of discussions with other students . . . ease-of-contact with the instructor . . . and in opportunities for expressing and sharing ideas" (p563-4). They also perceived a greater connection between the assignments and the course content. The authors suggest that the blended learning section encouraged more active learning, "a higher level of interaction between the student and the material," and "the sort of critical thinking sought by instructors – the creative application of assignments to course themes and content" (Pollock & Wilson, 2002, 564).

To reach Millennial students, the key for professors lies in finding a productive balance between lectures, active learning activities, and the effective integration of technology in supporting instruction. In a small-scale study at Pennsylvania State University, all twenty-five students surveyed expressed a preference for a combination of "50 percent lecturing and 50 percent interactive [learning activities]" (Roberts, 2005, 34). Interestingly, the students gave nearly equal ratings to the following three items when asked to rate their "importance to successful learning": the professor's "experience and expertise"; "ability to customize the class using the current technology available"; and "ability to professionally convey lecture points using contemporary software (for example, PowerPoint)" (Roberts, 2005, 34). Roberts noted that students in the study "expressed significant frustration with faculty members who simply transferred their lecture notes to PowerPoint slides and expected quality learning to occur" (36).

It would seem that if today's professors are to engage the students in their courses they will need to lecture less, use PowerPoint appropriately and with restraint, and embrace the possibilities offered by blended learning, multi-media, Web 2.0, and emerging learning technologies. When designing assignments, they might consider having students work collaboratively on multimedia presentations, webpages, wikis, or blogs. In class, for a visually literate generation used to multi-tasking and having a short attention span, multimedia may be an especially powerful teaching tool. As undergraduate student Carie Windham (2005) explains:

> the net Generation responds to a variety of media, such as television, audio, animation, and text. The use of a singular unit should be kept short and alternating, producing a class period as diverse in structure as it is in content. In my four years of courses, the best example . . . comes from a three-hour seminar I participated in on the Vietnam War. . . . Class began with a song from the period, and film clips were used throughout to illustrate key themes or replicate events. The lecture alternated discussion interspersed with photographs, tables, and graphics. (59)

Professors who search the Internet for teaching materials may find rich resources for designing assignments for students who prefer to learn through discovery rather than through lecture. Oblinger and Oblinger (2005) cite the example of *The Valley of the Shadow* online archive, which offers a collection of original records from a Confederate and a Union county during the Civil War, including "census data, agricultural records, newspaper articles, church records, and letters from soldiers and their families" (2.12).

Lectures and in-class discussions can also be enriched by thoughtful use of technology. For example, in a blended learning environment, professors can encourage students to continue in-class discussions on online discussion boards, an approach that might work especially well in large classes, in which students may be too shy to participate or simply not have the chance to do so given time constraints (McNeely, 2005). In large classes, an increasingly popular method for breaking up lectures, encouraging active learning, and providing instant feedback to students (and their professors) involves the use of clickers, hand-held devices that students use to respond to multiple-choice questions posted by the professor during class. Instantly, students can see the class's responses displayed on a large screen, and the professor can backtrack to deal with concepts that students appear to be struggling with. The instant response and elements of game-based learning embodied in the use of clickers may be especially appealing to the Millennial generation (Martyn, 2007). In a study comparing two sections of a course using clickers with two sections of the same course using discussion but no clickers, learning outcomes were comparable, but students in the clicker sections reported slightly more positive perceptions in terms of the value of clickers in improving understanding, increasing their sense of belonging, increasing interaction with peers and the instructor, and increasing their enjoyment of the course (Martyn, 2007).

Professors shouldn't assume that simply adding more technology to their courses will automatically engage Millennial learners. As Oblinger and Oblinger (2005) remind us, "It isn't technology per se that makes learning engaging for the Net Gen; it is the learning activity" (216). However they use technology, instructors should ensure that it is relevant and effectively integrated into the course (McNeely, 2005). In particular, they should think about how they can use technology as a tool to customize learning materials, offer increased convenience for students, and support collaborative learning (Oblinger & Oblinger, 2005). They should also keep in mind that their efforts are likely to be appreciated more highly by the older students in their courses than by the more critical Millennial students. Research on students' online learning experiences from the University of Central Florida found that, overall, the Net generation of students reported less "learning engagement" (73%) than their Gen-X (77%) or Boomer (85%) counterparts (Hartman, Moskal, & Dziuban, 2005). In particular, the Net Gen respondents in the study "felt that faculty response times lagged behind their expectations" (68). As Hartman et al. explain, while "Net Geners enjoyed the ability to form interactive communities among their peers. . . . [they] felt that the interaction mechanisms designed by their instructors were much less adequate than their personal technologies" (2005, 6.9). These researchers concluded that blended learning provides "the contact requested by Baby Boomers, the independence preferred by Gen-Xers, and the sense of community desired by Net Geners. Extensive use of e-mail, discussion groups, and live chat increases communication and collaboration among students and the instructor. (Hartman et al., 2005, 610)

5. Building on the positive and encouraging students' research skills

THE DISCUSSION OF THE MILLENNIAL GENERATION thus far may have left the impression of the Millennials as a group of spoiled, demanding students who are critical of the instruction they receive, who are prone to unsanctioned collaboration, and who are seeking "edutainment" rather than pursuing knowledge. However, such a characterization would be a distortion. In fact, Howe and Strauss describe today's students as hard working and pressured to do well; they compare the Millennial generation to Harry Potter's world, with its "group of kids who struggle to excel and have fun in a very structured institutional environment [and who] worry a lot about grades and exams and punishments and penalties" (107). Howe and Strauss note that Millennial students (at least those in the U.S.) tend to be smart, well rounded high achievers, who surpass preceding generations in the fields of math and science, which they tend to prefer over social sciences and humanities. Howe and Strauss praise them as "the most achievement-oriented collegians in [U.S.] history" and note that, "by the time they leave the campus gates, they may be the most learned and capable graduates ever" (144). To accommodate this generation, professors will have to make an effort to rethink how they approach instruction and consider how to positively channel these students' comfort with technology, preference for team work and collaborative learning, and desire to improve their communities.

However, despite this generation's ease with technology, professors shouldn't assume that they automatically know where and how to locate online journal articles and other credible scholarly sources for their papers. Nor should they simply forbid students from using the Internet for their research; after all, millions of scholarly sources are now available online. Rather, instructors must recognize the need to teach digital research skills to this generation of students, who may instinctively go to Wikipedia and Google (not Google Scholar) and may lack the skill to critically evaluate online sources. Professors at all levels should forge teaching partnerships with university librarians, who can offer hands-on workshops and direct students to helpful resources on research skills and evaluating sources. In first- and second-year courses, professors might also consider developing assignments targeting research skills, such as those described by Calkins and Kelley (2007).

Potential Pitfalls on the Road to Organizational Change

SHOULD UNIVERSITIES CHANGE to meet the needs of the Millennial generation? Absolutely. Like all organizations, universities must evolve as their environments and those they serve change. The change processes at universities will inevitably unfold at multiple levels, from professors adapting their teaching strategies to administrators managing strategic, infrastructural, and organizational change. However, dangers are sure to arise when administrators equate change – or simple imitation of their peer institutions – with progress. And other pitfalls lie in wait for administrators who handle change processes without adequate input from and regard for all stakeholders. As post-secondary institutions look at their strengths, weaknesses, opportunities, and threats – the venerable SWOT analysis – they frequently appear to underestimate that last quadrant: the potential pitfalls and risks that come with organizational change when it is not managed sensitively and intelligently. In my view, universities today face five key risks as they negotiate change, particularly when they become fixated on a student-as-consumer philosophy.

First, and perhaps most importantly, when what students want becomes a paramount consideration for university administrators, academic priorities may become distorted and universities may be drawn into a dangerous game in which they trade declines in the quality of their educational product for increases in student satisfaction ratings. In particular, as universities increase funding for student services at a rate that outpaces funding increases for instruction, universities may end up reducing course offerings, increasing class sizes, and eroding the quality of classroom instruction. Less obviously, universities catering to students' perceived demands may quietly move to remove long-standing curricular and other academic requirements, look the other way as grade inflation continues apace, and minimize penalties for plagiarism and other forms of academic misconduct, all in an effort to be more "student-friendly." In their study of academic misconduct in eleven Canadian universities, Christensen, Hughes and McCabe (2006) reported that when faculty members and teaching assistants were asked "what penalties a student would *most likely receive* if he or she was found guilty of cheating on a major test or assignment," 59% of the 1900 faculty respondents and 71% of the 683 TA respondents responded that such a student would most likely receive only a reprimand or a warning as opposed to a harsher penalty (14). If they allow such attitudes to prevail, universities must consider what they stand to lose in terms of the integrity of their degrees.

Second, as universities transform themselves, often adopting corporate models of administration ill-suited for the academy, they risk becoming increasingly hierarchical, less financially efficient, and perhaps even less effective in their delivery of services. And when certain student learning services are severed from the academic side of the university, those services can become academically impoverished as the bonds are cut that once tied them to the work lives of the academics who teach and do research. At the University of Calgary, the recent history of the Effective Writing Centre, established in 1978, provides a case in point. Once directed by an academic faculty member who kept abreast of research in the field and taught several credit courses in communication and writing each year, in 2009 the Centre (with no broad consultation or discussion) was moved from the Faculty of Communication and Culture (now part of the Faculty of Arts) to Student and Enrolment Services, where it will be managed by a full-time administrator who apparently will not be involved in research or in the teaching of credit courses in writing. While longer term outcomes remain to be seen, given its administrative (rather than faculty) designation, the newly created administrative position will undoubtedly be less attractive to potentially good candidates interested in combining administrative work with research and teaching in a tenure track position.

Third, when universities reinvent themselves, they often appear to do so without adequate research and planning, simply bulldozing existing services and structures and starting again at square one, throwing out the good with the bad, the helpful synergies and proven practices with those in need of rejuvenation. In the process, they may suffer an irreplaceable loss of institutional knowledge and memory and years of academic labour. Seldom, if ever, do administrators consider and account for such costs as they forge ahead with organizational change. And in universities' rush to make themselves over in the image of their peers – a move toward what theorists have called institutional "isomorphism" (DiMaggio & Powell, 1991, 66) – they risk losing many of the very things that made them unique and set them apart from their peers, making it harder for potential students to choose among competing universities on the basis of anything other than location.

Fourth, when universities negotiate the path to change in a top-down manner, foregoing consultation and discussion with key stakeholders, they can encourage public opposition and alienate the very groups they need as allies. For example, when the University of Toronto moved to adopt a flat-fee tuition scheme (discussed in more detail below), they were met with a lawsuit from the Arts and Science Students' Union, who argued that the decision-making process was flawed (Kershaw, 2009). And when universities drive through change without consulting with faculty and staff on the front lines, they risk alienating those upon whom they rely to serve the needs of students. When universities adopt a single-minded focus on the bottom line or on student engagement, staff and faculty engagement often gets trampled in the process, and the result can be diminished productivity and loyalty. This corrosive combination can eat away at the university from within and without as employees can be heard to say things like "I wouldn't send my kid here," potentially damaging universities' efforts at branding and selling themselves to their target student market (and their parents).

Finally, when universities use hefty tuition and fee increases to finance their transformation into more "student-friendly" environments, they stand to lose potentially good students and to consign the great majority of students to decades of student debt. Though Howe and Strauss (2003) predicted tuition price wars as universities would compete to attract Millennial students, the opposite trend seems to have emerged. Faced with common financial pressures and part of an oligopolistic educational marketplace, universities across Canada and the U.S. seem to be marching in lock step, increasing their tuition each year, adding mandatory fees, and refusing to undercut each other in a bid to attract more students on the basis of cost. According to both CAUT (2010) and the Delta Cost Project report (2010), over the past several years tuitions have continued to rise steadily and account for an ever-increasing share of university revenues in both the United States and Canada. Added to that, some universities have begun to implement mandatory student service fees; the proposed fee at the University of Alberta is pegged at $570 per year, equivalent to "a 10 percent increase in the cost of attending university" (Drolet, 2010, 1) while at the University of Calgary, a slightly lower but still substantial new student service fee is expected to bring millions more into the university coffers each year (Cooper, 2010).

These new fees are in addition to tuition increases, which in some programs are precipitous. At the University of Calgary, for example, the proposed tuition increases for professional programs such as business, law, medicine, and graduate-level engineering ranged from 17 to 32% (Drolet, 2010). And total tuition for the University's new eighteen-month Global Energy EMBA, a graduate degree in management, has been set at $105 000, a shocking price tag, even for a top-of-the-line program in which employers are expected to shoulder the cost (University of Calgary, 2010a). Another trend is the move toward flat-fee tuition, an approach adopted by the Faculty of Arts and Sciences at University of Toronto in 2009; under this new arrangement, expected to generate $14 million annually in additional tuition revenues, students taking three or four courses are compelled to pay the same amount as they would if they were taking five courses (Kershaw, 2009). Students choosing to work part-time to help finance a three-course load will end up having to pay close to $2000 more per year for their studies. The trends toward ever-increasing tuition rates and hefty mandatory fees ultimately reduce accessibility to higher education and threaten to widen the gap between the rich and the poor. At some point, universities must ask themselves whether more shiny new buildings and posh student spaces on campus are worth the potential longer-term social costs when an entire generation of students is saddled with mounting debt.

Conclusion

IT'S BEEN A DECADE since the Millennials first arrived on university campuses in Canada. Already this generation of students has left their mark indelibly on post-secondary institutions as they transform themselves, their buildings, their services, their philosophies, and their patterns of expenditure to cater to this generation of students. Many of these changes are positive and perhaps long overdue. However, if universities do not manage their change processes sensitively and intelligently, they risk losing more than they stand to gain. They must carefully consider the threats and risks as well as the perceived opportunities and benefits that may come with each new change.

In embracing change, universities should also embrace change processes that incorporate solid evidence-based research – as opposed to uncritical imitation of their peers or G-13 counterparts – and democratic and collegial decision-making processes that benefit from multiple perspectives reflecting a range of disciplinary expertise and a depth of practical experience and institutional memory. They should consider the dangers and pitfalls inherent in change that emanates by fiat from executive offices, and they should never overlook the value of genuine dialogue, consultation, discussion, persuasion, and consensus-building among all their stakeholder groups. As Leitzel,

Corvey, and Hiley (2004) caution, based on their experience guiding institutional change processes at the University of New Hampshire,

> Old ways of doing things must be explicitly analyzed and found wanting. Each suggestion and criticism must be viewed as legitimate. Preliminary decisions must be revisited when new information is presented. Decision-makers must spend more time listening than deciding. Moving ahead requires a reasonably high level of consensus. (2004, 42)

Leitzel *et al.* (2004) go on to recommend that, when considering change, university administrators should "design a process that is inclusive, connects visibly with the governance structure in place, and *over-represents* faculty" (43). Though such inclusive processes are time-consuming and fraught with possibilities for resistance, in the long-run they result in better decisions and move the university forward in a positive way for all stakeholders, from students and faculty to the community at large.

References

Calkins, S., & Kelley, M. R. (2007). Evaluating Internet and scholarly sources across the disciplines. Two case studies. *College Teaching, 55*(4), 151-156.

Canadian Association of University Teachers [CAUT]. (2010). *CAUT almanac of post-secondary education 2009-2010*. Retrieved from http://www.caut.ca/pages.asp?page=442

Christensen Hughes, J., & McCabe, D. L. (2006). Academic misconduct within higher education in Canada. *Canadian Journal of Higher Education, 36*(2), 1-21.

CTVglobemedia. (2010). *Globe Campus*. Retrieved July 15, 2010, from http://www.globecampus.ca/navigator/

Desrochers, D. M., Lenihan, C. M., & Wellman, J. V. (2010). *Trends in college spending 1998-2008: Where does the money come from? Where does it go? What does it buy?*. Washington DC. Delta Cost Project. Retrieved from http://www.deltacostproject.org/analyses/delta_reports.asp

DiMaggio, J., & Powell, W. W. (1991). Introduction. In W. W. Powell, & J. DiMaggio (Eds.), *The new institutionalism in organizational analysis*. Chicago. U of Chicago Press.

Drolet, D. (2010, March 8). Student fees set to rise. *University Affairs*. Retrieved from http://www.universityaffairs.ca/student-fees-set-to-rise.aspx

Greenberger, E., Lessard, J., Chen, C., & Farruggia, S. (2008). Self-entitled college students. Contributions of personality, parenting, and motivational factors. *Journal of Youth and Adolescence 37*, 1193-1204. doi. 10.1007/s10964-008-9284-9

Group of Thirteen (Canadian Universities). (2009). Wikipedia. Retrieved July 20, 2010, from http://en.wikipedia.org/wiki/Group_of_Thirteen_%28Canadian_universities%29

Hammer, K. (2010, July 8). A report card on cheating. Higher computer literacy, increased incidents of deceit. *Globe and Mail*, A 4.

HARTMAN, J., MOSKAL, P., & DZIUBAN, C. (2005). Preparing the academy of today for the learner of tomorrow. In D. G. Oblinger, & J. L. Oblinger (eds.) *Educating the Net generation.* (p6.1-6.15). Educause. Retrieved from http://www.educause.edu/educatingthenetgen

HOWE, N., & STRAUSS, W. (2003) *Millennials go to college: Strategies for a new generation on campus: recruiting and admissions, campus life, and the classroom.* Washington DC. American Association of Collegiate Registrars and Admissions Officers and LifeCourse Associates.

JONES, C., & RAMANAU, R. (2009). Collaboration and the Net generation. The changing characteristics of first year university students. *CSCL 2009 Proceedings*, 237-241.

KERSHAW, A. (2009, June 15). U of T switches to controversial flat-fee tuition. *University Affairs.* Retrieved from http://www.universityaffairs.ca/u-of-t-switches-to-controversial-flat-fee-tuition.aspx

LEITZEL, J., CORVEY, C., & HILEY, D. (2004). Integrated planning and change management at a research university. *Change*, January/February, 37-43.

MARTYN, M. (2000). Clickers in the classroom. An active learning approach. *Educause Quarterly Magazine, 30*(2), 71-74. Retrieved from http://net.educause.edu/ir/library/pdf/EQM0729.pdf

MCNEELY, B. (2005). Using technology as a learning tool, not just the cool new thing. In D. G. Oblinger, & J. L. Oblinger (eds.) *Educating the Net generation.* (p4.1-4.10). Educause. Retrieved from http://www.educause.edu/educatingthenetgen

OBLINGER, D. G., & OBLINGER, J. L. (2005). Is it age or IT. First steps toward understanding the Net generation. In D. G. Oblinger, & J. L. Oblinger (eds.) *Educating the Net generation.* (p2.1-2.20) Educause. Retrieved from http://www.educause.edu/educatingthenetgen

POLLOCK, H., & WILSON, B. M. (2002). Evaluating the impact of Internet teaching. Preliminary evidence from American national government classes. *Political Science & Politics, 35*(3), 561-566. doi:10.1017/S1049096502000847

PRENSKY, M. (2001). Digital natives, digital immigrants. *On the Horizon,* 9(5). MCB University Press.

ROBERTS, G. (2005). Technology and learning expectations of the Net generation. In D. G. Oblinger, & J. L. Oblinger (eds.) *Educating the Net generation.* (p3.1-3.7) Educause. Retrieved from http://www.educause.edu/educatingthenetgen

ROOSEVELT, M. (2009, February 17). Student expectations seen as causing grade disputes. *New York Times.* Retrieved from http://www.nytimes.com/2009/02/18/education/18college.html?_r=2

SPECTRE, M., & PRENSKY, M. (n.d.). *Theoretical underpinnings of Games2train's approach.* Retrieved July 19, 2010, from http://www.games2train.com/site/html/theory.html

SOWDEN, C. (2005). Plagiarism and the culture of multilingual students in higher education abroad. *ELT Journal,* 59(3), 226-233.

UNIVERSITY OF CALGARY HASKAYNE SCHOOL OF BUSINESS. (2010a). *Global energy EMBA.* Retrieved July 16, 2010, from http://www.energyemba.com/

UNIVERSITY OF CALGARY OFFICE OF INSTITUTIONAL ANALYSIS. (2010b). *Fact book 2009-2010.* Retrieved from http://www.oia.ucalgary.ca/system/files/2009-2010FB.pdf

WINDHAM, C. (2005) The student's perspective. In D. G. Oblinger, & J. L. Oblinger (eds.) *Educating the Net generation.* (p5.1-5.16). Educause. Retrieved from http://www.educause.edu/educatingthenetgen

A Fifty-year Dialogue with Students and Science

Cooper H. Langford III

A Few Notes on my own Education

I WAS THE SON OF A PROFESSOR of symbolic logic with a richly logical sense of humour and a mother who emphasized the importance of language. As a consequence of my mother's multiple sclerosis, I spent my adolescence in the household of an uncle who led corporations engaged with images in one way or another (film, overhead projection, etc.). My father was the dedicated specialist, ignoring the outside world, and my uncle the articulate generalist, very much engaged with a broad world. I was lucky enough to study chemistry first at Harvard where of sixteen courses required for an 'AB' (the only degree from the college) only five-and-a-half were required to be in chemistry. This left a lot of intellectual room and the college had a well-defined structure for general education. I went on to graduate study at Northwestern where a fairly didactic presentation of science characterized courses, as it had in chemistry at Harvard. Of course, the key experience of Ph.D. study was research apprenticeship. I obtained an NSF Post-doctoral fellowship, which I took to London in the University College department led by Sir Christopher Ingold. In Ingold's department the weekly seminar displayed Ingold's ability to start from any presentation and carry forward a discussion that created ideas eventually far from the topic of the presentation. All of us juniors struggled and competed to imitate what he did to build on ideas and create. I see this as a crucial step in the final stage of the education and apprenticeship of a scientific researcher, that it requires experience in a highly creative research institution.

The Formative Experience at Amherst

GOING AGAINST THE ADVICE of my Ph.D. supervisor, Robert Burwell, and my Post-doctoral mentor, Sir Ronald Nyholm, I elected to take up an appointment at Amherst College in Massachusetts. Amherst is one of the elite liberal arts colleges focused on undergraduates that enrich the American system. The advice against my choice turned on the absence of graduate students, who are the eyes and hands of experimental research. It was assumed that Amherst would stunt my research development. My choice flowed from my father's model. I didn't want to become narrowly focused on research in his style; I wanted to be sure to 'teach'.

Amherst in the early 1960s was an excellent place to learn to be a teacher. In contrast to many universities, it did not hand assignments to new appointees and assume they could cope. Team teaching was a prominent part of the program, partly from necessity since there were no graduate teaching assistants. The College's philosophy encouraged most senior and distinguished professors to teach large introductory courses. My initial assignments included working with Ralph Beebe in the introductory chemistry course and on a team led by Arnold Arons in the required first year course for all students in the college, Science 1. Science 1 was a combined introduction to physics and calculus. Most of the physical scientists taught discussion sections of the physics part and mathematicians and physicists taught the mathematics sections. The whole staff met weekly to consider the presentation of the next topics.

The approach of Science 1 was historical and cultural without any concessions limiting the rigour needed by science students. This was physics taught as a liberal art. In every case, the historical material was used to show the logic of the addition to knowledge and reasons for consensus to converge on what we now regard as central. In this sense, it was imperfect history. It was rather in the style called 'whig history' where the ideas regarded as sound by modern scientists get all the attention at the price of ignoring much of the cultural/intellectual temper of the times of discovery and the overall profile of the discoverers. I have argued that this whig history approach at least captures an argument that did convince scientists at some time and is, therefore, a way to teach from a discovery approach. In our textbook, *The Development of Chemical Principles*, this discovery approach is characterized as follows:

> We hope that the reader can participate in this development to 'rediscover' . . . theory for himself (sic) and, at least vicariously, practice science. We also hope it will be apparent that . . . the last word has . . . not been said . . . We [further] try to follow the longer-range development of fruitful ideas to show that a good theoretical idea evolves.[1]

The discovery approach has been subjected to much discussion in the science teaching community. At the university level at least implementation has been rare. For a course like Science 1 that was intended for a broad audience 'discovery' certainly offers more for the non-major student to carry forward over many years, not [mainly] because it presents history, but because it reveals the practice of science and its debates.

The difficulty is that the practice of modern science depends in large measure on abstractions and idealizations that are not intuitive and are difficult for most students. For this reason, the laboratory in Science 1 devoted the first three weeks to the 'dull' pastime of watching a cart roll down a track. The position vs. time data were transcribed on to graph paper and various interpretations, such as for velocity, undertaken. Finally such interpretations were abstracted into simple, necessarily approximate, mathematical expressions that were useful idealizations. These are the steps essential to the transformation of viewpoint required to pass from Aristotelian physics to the modern view commonly associated with Galileo and his contemporaries. This is the transformation that remains difficult for contemporary beginners.

Teaching on the staff of Science 1 led me to the conviction that we needed to reform the introduction to chemistry to meet the expectations of students who had completed that course. The textbook cited above was the outcome of the effort to develop a systematic discovery-oriented approach to chemistry. It was adopted in several other liberal arts colleges, but has had only a few uses in larger universities. It was a critical success, as evidenced by the fact that it was brought out in Dover reprint in their classics series in 1995. Most introductory chemistry instruction sticks to a didactic presentation of ideas the students are expected to assimilate without much justification and then show that they can manipulate.

The Unresolved Tension

THOMAS KUHN's *The Structure of Scientific Revolutions* was published in 1962. It has been described as the most cited book in the social sciences of the 20th century.[2] One of the strengths of the comparatively small Amherst faculty was regular cross-disciplinary interaction. The book was promptly taken up by a multi-disciplinary faculty reading group. My first comment on Kuhn was that I wasn't sure that he had a fully convincing reading of the history of science but that he surely understood science education. In Kuhn's view, science education is a process of indoctrination of students into current paradigms. Kuhn can be construed as justifying the standard didactic presentation of the current status of a science to students and challenging them to work within the paradigm by solving the exercises presented at the ends of chapters. Mastery of the paradigm and the capacity to work within it comes before exploration of its basis. Indeed, the latter step may not be necessary for the effective practice of science. Nevertheless, students who complete the training and apprenticeship to become researchers learn that extension of a paradigm, or the challenging of it, requires skill in debate and assimilation of the twin demands for novelty and scepticism that Merton and Ziman identified as norms of science.[3]

Elaborating the inference that Kuhn's analysis supports the didactic presentation depends on the question of familiarity. Must a student acquire some manipulative familiarity before it is possible to appreciate the internal logic of the paradigm? If there is a tacit element to the knowledge a student of science must acquire, then the presentation of behaviour models and setting of practice exercises that will be corrected by a 'coach' reflects a standard way to transfer tacit knowledge.[4] The tacit knowledge may centre on exactly the shift of cognitive style to assimilate the abstraction and idealization behind modern scientific reasoning. The change from Aristotle to Galileo was a recognized Kuhnian revolution. Kuhn argues such paradigm shifts are similar to 'gestalt' shifts. Perhaps each new student of science must achieve a personal 'gestalt' shift. This is clearly the eventual outcome of conventional didactic science education. A proponent of "discovery" approaches must find a route to the tacit shift. Aarons' intensive, repetitive use of conversion of a simple bench top experience into graphs and equations in the Science 1 lab represents one attempt to accomplish the shift promptly. This argument for didactic paradigm inculcation is not necessarily persuasive. There is no clear demonstration of the failure of discovery teaching, nor can the argument against it be dismissed out of hand. For me, the tension between the two has remained unresolved. However, 'facts' fade from memory. The one thing that seems clear and easily demonstrated by the experience of most of us is that the didactic method leaves little long term residue for the student who does not continue in a field, whereas the discovery method may leave a more enduring impression of what a scientific discipline has to offer. Discovery does try to introduce the 'practice of science.' In my view this strongly recommends discovery for meeting the needs of the so-often-overlooked 'non-major' in the class.

Research as a Teaching Tool

IF THE GOAL OF DISCOVERY TEACHING is to simulate the practice of science, then we should consider practice itself. Another classic mode of transmission of tacit knowledge is the apprenticeship mode. The assumption is often made that a student at an elementary level does not have the necessary background and tools to participate in creative research. Such an assumption is less often made about students of humanities and social sciences. The human sciences are seen as closer to the life experience of students; thus students are encouraged to engage issues in a critical fashion quite early in their careers. At Calgary, for example, a recent effort in the interdisciplinary Communication and Culture unit involved the introduction of a series of first -year seminars that were devoted to research. These are offered to small groups of students, each group led by a senior professor on a topic drawn from that professor's area of scholarly activity. This effort is characterized as an introduction to the core of what university education is about. Similar experiences in most natural sciences seem harder to construct, but probably not impossible. I made a bit of an attempt in my teaching of introductory chemistry at Carleton where I constructed term paper assignments. These were a sort of 'synthetic research topic' using historical data but carefully selected so that the students could carry out an analysis using no tools that were too 'sophisticated'. It was considered quite novel to have a term paper in a first year chemistry course.

Summer research experiences and final (Honours) year projects are well established practices. However, these tend to be reserved for more advanced students. This misses an important educational opportunity. My experience,[*] especially in liberal arts colleges, indicates that it is possible to integrate students in earlier years into research programs. The active challenges of research and the contact with more senior research students and researchers provide a rich climate for tacit learning and can foster attitudinal changes that convert a competent

* The leader of a national research network once remarked in a network meeting I attended: "[This research group] does with master's students what we do with post-docs". A member very familiar with the group commented *sotto voce*: "master's students? . . . they include undergraduates."

student into an outstanding one. Unhappily, a large university cannot offer engagement in active research programs to all students who might benefit. But at least it can make efforts to increase the availability of research opportunities. As well, it can make efforts, as Calgary currently does, to recognize and publicize undergraduate research. This can, at least, call the attention of undergraduates to the role research plays in individual learning.

Student Advising

IN LARGE UNIVERSITIES, providing academic advice has moved far from the life of most frontline teachers. Partly this has been a question of workload and partly it has been a product of concern with ensuring that rules are accurately interpreted. This is unfortunate. Many come into the university because they have learned that a university degree is a necessary credential to enter the types of careers they aspire to follow. No doubt, this is a rational consideration, but it should not be the only one. Students in this position and some others drift through their programs with little sense of the overall purpose of the required work.

In my time at Carleton, I had the opportunity to act as the founding director of a program called 'Integrated Science Studies.' It was a program in the Faculty of Science but it did not require a conventional major. If the metaphor for the majors was a set of parallel lines, then this program sought to open possibilities for lines crossing diagonally. (It also required a coherent set of three courses outside the sciences to be chosen.) The planners (I was on the committee) saw this as something students would recognize and seek, often from the first year. As the program developed, almost no students identified it in first year. Rather, I found myself approached by students entering second year who had gone through first year and were confused about 'why they were in university.' The process of planning a self-designed unconventional program provided the experience of analysis of an overall set of educational goals.

It seems to me critical for active scholars to be involved in the advising process in order to help students understand what a university is about and why they are there. Otherwise too many will drift through thinking only in terms of accumulating credits toward the certificate A brave experiment at Calgary was the movement a few yeas ago to insist that every program compile an 'explicit syllabus' that would document the relationships of the various courses required or recommended and articulate the philosophy that underlay the curriculum. Somehow, the point of the exercise didn't get through to most faculty and the resulting documents have faded into obscurity. Perhaps it was too ambitious. Perhaps it was trying to codify much that was tacit, but it represents an approach worth revisiting and linking more closely to some increase of face-to-face discussions around it.

An Externalist View of Science

FOR THE LAST TEN YEARS I have been teaching in the Science, Technology and Society program. I developed a course called 'Science in Society.' I find little resistance to the idea that working toward an understanding of the workings of science in our society is an important enterprise in our world. There is less appreciation of the reverse thrust of the title, how our society influences the science we get and why it is finally a social process to generate these spectacular examples of reliable knowledge. The one faculty in the university that has unexpectedly ignored this enterprise in large measure is the Faculty of Science.

Thus, the key question I want to address here is the role of an externalist view of science in the education of scientists.

I first taught this area in a seminar for Honours students in chemistry at Carleton in the 1970s. Scholarship in the field has expanded tremendously since. At the time I characterized it as an examination of some issues in the history and sociology of science. A recent McGill University Dean of Science (a Carleton alumnus) once publicly characterized this as the most valuable course of his undergraduate career. I'll use this as a springboard from which to launch my argument for the importance for a science student to examine this external analysis of science.

Early sociologists of science, among whom Robert Merton is the heroic figure, examined the behaviour of scientific communities without examining scientific ideas *per se*. They revealed a number of practices that it is valuable for scientists to appreciate explicitly. A good example is the description of the 'Mathew effect,' a metaphor for the tendency for the better known scientist to receive the major credit for the work of a team. Another important insight recognizes the differences in editorial philosophy that account for the differences in journal rejection rates experienced by researchers across the spectrum from the physical sciences to the humanities. The history of scientific publication clarifies the odd impersonal tone of scientific writing as originating with editors' efforts to get scientific debate under control so that it could be most fruitful, not from some abstract concept of the uncommitted scientist speaking in the voice of nature.[5]

Scholarship, again since the publication of Thomas Kuhn's *The Structure of Scientific Revolutions*, has turned attention to the content of science itself. Kuhn's analysis made it clear that a simple linear progressive model of the advance of science is inadequate. Work on the founders of the scientific revolution has identified the theological echoes in the term 'natural law', helping to explain why we find the term law fading in everyday scientific use in favour of terms like model. A next stage of analysis of the social native sciences originates from an anthropological exploration of scientific culture. It has illuminated the role of rhetoric in science. It is acceptable to admit that we write to persuade because scientific facts are the outcome of settling controversies and the emphasis in this approach on the role of things clarifies how we speak for our materials, apparatus and experiments. In the late and unlamented 'science wars', some scientists expressed fear that this sociological analysis would turn students away from science. My experience is the reverse. Emerging scientists recognize themselves and their colleagues in this and find it stimulating.

The Scientist as a Member of the Community

Finally, a scientific education should examine the role of a scientist in broader communities. Here it is important to address the significance of expertise and the obligations of science with respect to the larger goals of society. One danger of the didactic approach to teaching science is to construct a picture of expertise as involving a clear method to obtain 'the right answer'. Too often a scientist slips into the error of thinking that any scientist would address a given problem the same way and that the rest of the world need only understand what scientists have to say. The presence of credible scientists in all political parties is enough to show the limits of this attitude. As a former student of mine, John Carey, now executive director of Environment Canada's National Water Research Institute puts it to his scientific colleagues: "science isn't policy." Somewhere this point needs to arise in a scientific education. Perhaps this is an added argument for including the externalist examination of science in the curriculum. Our colleagues in engineering do require some study of the social aspects of technology for professional certification.

Scientists also need to realize that the resources provided for scientific research by the society vastly exceed the levels made available to areas of knowledge of predominantly cultural significance. There is an instrumental goal in society's support of science. In the context of a discipline and the charm of extending its paradigm, it is important to realize that solutions to problems, externally posed, are expected. Examination of the history of science shows that such expectations are not always at odds with advance of fundamental knowledge. Donald Stokes book, *Pasteur's Quadrant*[6], points out that Pasteur's work on problems of the wine and milk producers led to the development of the foundations of microbiology and that this is not an isolated incident. There must finally be a balance between the disciplinary claims of what is sometimes called the republic of science and the claims of its sponsors. It is wise for science education to include some analyses of the process of innovation. It is not as simple as making a 'discovery', getting a patent and 'commercializing', and it is not limited to supporting markets.

Concluding Remark

I HAVE ATTEMPTED TO REVIEW the series of issues raised by teaching in the university with the special mandate to teach chemistry. I have included my analysis of the cognitive challenges of teaching science, the role beyond the classroom of the significance of the university as a research institution, guiding students' programs, and going beyond the boundaries of the disciplines. I believe the goal that unifies this discussion is an effort to achieve liberal education through the sciences. I'll end with a quotation from my Amherst mentor, Arnold Arons, mentioned above: "[He] can teach baseball statistics as a liberal art." It's not in the specific subject but in the intellectual approach that learning lies.

Endnotes

1   C.H. LANGFORD AND R.A. BEEBE, "The Development of Chemical Principles" Addison-Wesley, Reading, Ma, 1969. (Dover reprint edition, 1995)

2   Curiously, it is not so well known in natural science communities.

3   JOHN ZIMAN, *Reliable Knowledge,* Cambridge University Press, Cambridge, 1978, and Robert.K. Merton (1942) "The Normative Structure of Science". Reprinted in Merton, Robert K. *The Sociology of Science: Theoretical and Empirical Investigations* University of Chicago Press, Chicago, 1979. .

4   I. NONAKA AND H. TAKEUCHI, *The Knowledge Creating Company,* Oxford Press, New York 1995.

5   The candid 1968 account of the tortuous path to a major scientific result in James D. Watson's *The Double Helix* Atheneum, NY, with his account of all the full spectrum emotions that he and his colleagues experienced made clear, as one newspaper put it, that "scientists are human after all".

6   DONALD STOKES, *Pasteur's Quadrant,* Brookings Institution, Washington, DC, 1997.

Thoughts on Interdisciplinarity
A Mature Student's Journey

James Butler

EDUCATION – ALL EDUCATION – should be transformative. Perhaps that is the singular difference between education and training. To be transformed is not only to see the world differently but to be in the world differently. While many disciplines enrich knowledge and equip students to become professionals, the processes through which this knowledge is delivered can isolate a student within a specific paradigm that both informs and inhibits at the same time. Disciplinary concentration becomes specialized knowledge that is distilled and narrowed into deeper silos buried far below the horizon. They may offer an occasional glimpse of other realities but that is not the norm. Graduate students, in particular, become sequestered in ivory dungeons making sense of the external world through what Petrie (1976) describes as their "cognitive maps." Their specialized or even overspecialized knowledge can mean, "Two opposing disciplinarians can look at the same thing and not see the same thing."

The interdisciplinary model for education can prevent over-segmentation and loss of interconnectedness by building networks of knowledge that coalesce into a carefully integrated system incorporating a blend of perspectives. For this to work there has to be a catalyst that brings coherence by avoiding a collapse into a myriad of disconnected ideas and unfocused insights. That catalyst is the individual student because the interdisciplinary model offers an enhanced academic experience that must be navigated with considerable self-discipline.

This does mean that there is a clear need for a mentoring process that offers the student access to a critical support system. Ideally this system is a combination of peer mentors and professors.

Yet what passes for interdisciplinarity in some institutions is in fact a multi-disciplinary model in which a variety of disciplines are used in support of each other or to resolve problems through narrow areas of relevant knowledge. Petrie (1976) writes:

> It is that multidisciplinary projects simply require everyone to do their own thing together with little or no necessity for any one participant to be aware of any other participant's work. Perhaps a project director or manager is needed to glue the final product together, but the pieces are fairly clearly of disciplinary size and shape. Interdisciplinary efforts, on the other hand, require more or less integration and even modification of the disciplinary subcontributions while the inquiry is proceeding. Different participants need to take into account the contributions of their fellows in order to make their own contribution.

Harris (2006) offers the following distinction between the multi-disciplinary model and the interdisciplinary:

> Multidisciplinary or multi-professional: learning together, groups of students from different professions learning common content.
>
> Interdisciplinary or inter-professional: shared learning, learning together to promote collaborative practice.

A simple way of illustrating this is the construction of a house, which requires the participation of a host of trades each of which contributes to the overall construction of the building while remaining separate and distinct from all others. People operating heavy equipment prepare the site. Concrete framers build the forms and masons pour the foundation. Carpenters frame the house so that the electricians and plumbers can begin their installations. Each succeeding trade works separately from the others and while there is interconnectedness, their contributions remain separate and distinct from each other. There is a compartmentalization that sustains the notion of specialization. In complete contrast to this, interdisciplinary knowledge aims to reduce the barriers between and within disciplines by drawing on specific knowledge in unique and non-standard ways. It offers a variety of lenses to the individual in an attempt to overcome what may well be an embedded form of tunnel vision that inhibits thinking and restricts the ability to navigate and make sense of increasingly complex social worlds. My experiences with the former Faculty of Communication and Culture at the University of Calgary have given me a much greater appreciation for the true value of the interdisciplinary model both to the academy and to society in general. These experiences have led me to embrace "integration" and "collaborative practice" as the essence of interdisciplinarity.

When I was first asked to contribute an essay to this collection I hesitated, because I was in the middle of fieldwork for my PhD dissertation and I was uncertain that I could spare the time. But then I recognized that I actually needed to take some time to reflect on the academic journey I had begun in earnest some eight years prior. The interdisciplinary approach prevailed throughout my graduate studies. My introduction to interdisciplinary studies began at the University of Calgary when I enrolled in a part-time course with a general notion that I might finally complete the undergraduate degree I had initially started in 1967. I had never completely abandoned the pursuit; I simply had not found a course of studies that fit me. Over the years I had taken English courses, studied the history of Southeast Asia, upgraded my calculus mark and even dabbled in business with the encouragement and financial support of my employer. At one point with a family to support and needing to earn a better living I enrolled in a three-year computer science program at a local community college in Newfoundland. That decision took me into the world of Information Technology and connected me to a career that offered me the opportunity to interact with a variety of situations in which my main function was to identify and resolve problems. I believe it was here that I finally found value for my rather eclectic thinking models that often see patterns others may not. For me the world of people is a complex set of systems that interact, intertwine, fuse, and disintegrate. Reality is negotiated, realized, altered and destabilized. Following those patterns and making sense of them is only possible when the observer can call on flexible and perhaps intuitive ways of thinking. It is not a specialist who is best suited to this undertaking but rather a generalist; one who has been equipped with a hybrid set of perspectives and insights drawn simultaneously from multiple disciplines. There is a sense of collaboration inherent in the interdisciplinary model in that those who follow this practice draw extensively from a range of disciplines each of which contributes to something greater than possible in any one area of specialization.

The notion of collaboration constitutes the primary experience that I had both as an undergraduate and now as a graduate student at the University of Calgary. My own journey through interdisciplinary studies serves as an instructive model of how it is possible to combine a breadth of knowledge with sufficient depth so as to provide a unique and rich education, one that prepares the individual for numerous possible careers in almost any discipline but just as importantly helps to foster the kind of informed citizen so essential to any modern society. I chose "no area of concentration" in my Bachelor of Arts. Thus I was able to maximize the breadth of my studies and to incorporate a wide range of disciplines into my degree. Two of the courses that I took after I returned to school in January 2001 helped to shape my thinking in critical ways.

I had enrolled in the Weekend U program intending to pursue the three-year Bachelor of General Studies. My first course was General Studies 357: Change Management. At the time I was working as a consultant in the Information Technology industry and change management, as I then understood it, was very much a part of my work-life. I had spent the previous decade implementing the flood of new technologies that were transforming the workplace so my preconceptions were firmly entrenched. The actual course was an entirely different experience. It was in fact transformative. The standard model of change management that I had encountered in my professional life was one that focused on the general goal of achieving a desired corporate goal by mitigating any disruptions that might emerge from resistance to a preset plan of action. Thus it was not so much about managing change as it was managing people. But in the course we began by exploring the impact change has on the individual so as to understand how group dynamics must allow for the needs of the individual and to see those as opportunities to learn rather than incidents to be mitigated. One critical task that we each had to complete was to maintain a journal in which we reflected on our experiences in the course and how we integrated these into our own lives.

The goal was to document both our intellectual and our emotional journeys. In the end we were required to analyse our journals and it became obvious to me that over time I stopped trying to separate the two. I discovered that the process of intellectual growth is tightly coupled with my emotions and that learning is always as much an emotionally driven process as it is an intellectual one. This was a profound shift for me.

All of my life I had struggled with my emotional responses to intellectual challenges and learning. Now I had discovered that my emotions were not a problem or an impediment. Rather it was my own misunderstanding of the place of my emotions in my intellectual journey that got in the way. Through the work I did in this course I came to understand that my emotions afford an essential lens through which I can engage and understand the issues and ideas I encounter. This integration of emotional and intellectual intelligence is essential to interdisciplinary education in that it supports the inclusion of the whole person into the learning model. It rejects any trace of the positivism or scientism that may impede a more complex and nuanced worldview and following Foucault completes the task of decentring the knowing subject. Dislodged from the safe perch of an objective and detached observation post we are left to swim in the tidal currents of new and sometimes contradictory ideas. Thus my introduction to interdisciplinary education opened up a new way of knowing or perhaps more correctly allowed me to understand how I learned best and that what once seemed to be a problem might actually be a gift.

Subsequently, I moved from a course that helped me to learn how to learn to one that exposed me to an ocean of ideas. I began the full-year course in General Studies 300. I have always had a need to make sense of the world and it was in this course that I recognized what I was actually trying to make sense of was a human construct and not a natural state. The journey from Plato and Aristotle by way of Marcus Aurelius and Epictetus to Kant and Hegel might seem to some to be of historical interest but of limited value in our modern world of mass media and the twenty-four hour news cycle. Taking time to actually reflect on the larger questions that gave rise to philosophy and religion might seem to some as being at best quaint. Yet what I encountered was something far different. What I came to know was that the need to make sense of our very existence is not some esoteric project for impractical people. It is the essence of our being. Our need to know and to understand has always been with us and always will be. That we will never truly complete that project must not impede us. Instead it should motivate us to continue, knowing that others like us will take up the task in their time. That insight led me to raise my own sights. With the enthusiastic encouragement of a professor, who herself had returned to the academy as a mature student, I decided that rather than settling for a BGS I would pursue an Honours BA in Communications Studies. This was a big leap and at the time I really did not think that I would go further than that and yet I did. This foundation was an extraordinary experience that guided me into graduate studies, first at Memorial University in Newfoundland and then back to the University of Calgary.

After completing a Master's of Philosophy in Humanities at Memorial University in St. John's I accepted an offer from the then Faculty of Communication and Culture to undertake studies for a PhD. I enrolled in the new Culture and Society division. My interest in identity construction was seen as a more suitable fit for that area and this decision did lead me to take a far different direction in my studies than I had originally envisioned. My original proposal was designed to explore the construction of online extended families through genealogical research that was conducted over the Internet and that involved people from across North America and Western Europe with a connection to my home province of Newfoundland and Labrador. However, in my first year of studies I became aware of a far more intriguing topic when I learned that the Mi'kmaq of Newfoundland, whose existence as an Indigenous people has long been officially denied, were in the process of gaining official recognition under the Indian Act. It was obvious to me that this was a relevant and important topic, one that has significance for the nation as well as for the province of Newfoundland and Labrador. This alone was not sufficient to convince me to change my thesis topic. That decision really came from an accumulation of insights and ideas that I gained from my course work in my first year of graduate studies. Two graduate courses had particular significance in this. Each of them opened up areas of thought that I had not previously explored.

In my International and Intercultural Communications course I was exposed to critical insights about how ideas may be shared across divergent cultures and societies. What was most profoundly important for me in this course was to learn how colonization is more about people than resources. Long after the exploiters have left, the legacy of oppression that has been inculcated into the colonized often remains, leaving a world apparently trapped in destitution and privation. Those of us who stand outside of this historical experience often observe it from the perspective of privilege and this position of power acts to distort our understanding of the struggles undertaken by the colonized to construct better lives and better futures. This is not to minimize the problems and challenges faced by many in the so-called Third World. It is instead to reframe the idea that they need us to resolve their problems for them. What I learned from this course was that we must learn to listen to those voices, to the wisdom of the oppressed. We must understand that we collectively construct our worlds through language and ideas. When we fail to hear the words of the oppressed we continue to impose our world-construct on them. We continue to colonize them.

The continued colonization of the oppressed was made evident to me through the second course, Development Studies, Conceptual Approaches. The theoretical content of this course really was secondary to the experience of travelling to Jaipur, capital of Rasjasthan State, India both to attend an international symposium on development and while there also to conduct research. As Latimer et al. (1999) note, "In designing a course, there is a creative tension between providing relevant information and promoting experiential learning." While there are many valuable insights that I have gained through my immersion in interdisciplinary learning models at all levels of my academic studies, few match the lived experience of being present with the people most directly relevant to a course of studies and to be opened up to their worldview and lives by being literally on the ground with them. I came away from that experience a profoundly altered person, one who recognized that it is not sufficient that we study the world. We must acknowledge that in that act we also transform it and thus must seek to shape outcomes in positive directions. We cannot simply appropriate the knowledge and experiences of others through our research. We must also give back to those whose knowledge we seek to collect and study. We must also be conscious that through our presence we bring change that may be both disruptive and constructive and thus we must act deliberately so as to ensure that outcomes meet the aims and needs of those whose worlds we intrude upon. That commitment to a certainty of purpose informed my decision to work with a professor and a group of graduate and undergraduate students to form an NGO designed to provide aid and support to women in the rural areas of Rajasthan State in India. These outcomes might have been possible within a different pedagogical model; however, in my experience what is unique to the interdisciplinary model is that such outcomes are not only supported and encouraged, they are expected.

Throughout my time with Communication and Culture there has been a clear arc that has guided my path through my studies. This has not been a rigid model framed by a positivist worldview. Instead it has provided me with the ability to be adaptive and flexible in my thinking. I now embrace the idea that there is much wisdom to be earned from those with whom I seek to study. I have learned that I am an inductive thinker, one who sees patterns and relationships that may not be evident or relevant to others. While I understand this to be a personal strength I am also aware that this way of thinking can keep me unfocused and incoherent in my work. However, there is great discipline in the interdisciplinary model when it is used effectively. It has helped me to be open to the opportunities engendered through my eclectic bent while being disciplined enough to narrow my vision to manageable projects. In addition, because I have been exposed to multiple models of interconnected research practices, rather than enter a field of study with pre-packaged concepts and theories, I have learned that I can carry out empirical research that begins from an inductive model so that I do not automatically apply the filters that are inherent to deductive reasoning. Thus the single most important lesson that I have learned over these past several years is that I must remain open to all of the possibilities that lie before me. There are endless ways of knowing the world and each is a unique and often profoundly different experience. As an academic who seeks to become a scholar, I believe that my immersion into an interdisciplinary milieu has opened me to integrating my research with human needs and building a collaborative scholarly practice.

References

HARRIS, B. (2006). 2006 Pauline Cerasoli Lecture. Interdisciplinary education⸱ what, why, and when?. *Journal of Physical Therapy Education*, 20(2), 3-8. Retrieved from CINAHL Plus with Full Text database.

LATIMER, E., DEAKIN, A., INGRAM, C., O'BRIEN, L., SMOKE, M., & WISHART, L. (1999). An interdisciplinary approach to a day-long palliative care course for undergraduate students. *CMAJ: Canadian Medical Association Journal*, 161(6), 729-731. Retrieved from Academic Search Complete database.

PETRIE, HUGH. (1976). Do you see what I see? The epistemology of interdisciplinary inquiry. *Journal of Aesthetic Education, Vol. 10, No. 1,* pp. 29-43. University of Illinois Press. Retrieved from Jstor database.

The Student Experience
What It's Worth

Dalmy Baez

WHEN I WAS SEVENTEEN YEARS OLD and about to graduate from high school, I was offered a substantial scholarship to enter a business program at a technical institute. I was quite excited about the prospect, knowing that few others were granted such an opportunity. I recall sharing the news enthusiastically with one of my high school teachers. But before I could finish, he interrupted me, saying "you're not considering going somewhere other than university are you?" Shocked, I asked what the difference was. Although he did not give me a precise answer, I remember distinctly just how certain he was about his advice to attend university: there was nothing wrong with a technical institute or a college, he said, "but *you* are built for university, built for that atmosphere and environment . . . trust me on this one." He told me that if I didn't go I would regret it. So I decided to take his advice and register at the University of Calgary.

As I write this essay five years later, I know that my teacher's advice served me well. As I try to recall the whole experience, from the first day to convocation, I feel as if these last five years have been like running some gargantuan marathon. I will describe this journey year by year, offering both highlights and low points, to share the most valuable aspect of each particular year.

First Year:
A taste of loneliness and freedom

"You mean they don't have detention in university?"

THE TRANSITION FROM HIGH SCHOOL to University is by no means seamless. In fact, coming out of high school to University I felt like a toddler just learning to walk, suddenly expected to run a hundred-metre sprint. There was no one to choose my courses for me, no one to provide me with textbooks and no one to pay my fees. I was daunted by the sheer size of the institution. I found myself walking in circles and often accidentally entering the wrong classroom for lack of familiarity with the buildings. In fact, I recall one day wandering in the food court, close to tears because I had been looking for the fee office for almost an hour. I was lucky to find another one of my high school teachers in the hallway who knew the campus and kindly pointed me in the right direction.

For the first few weeks I was overwhelmed by loneliness and confusion. It was different from any other school I had attended. I recognized only a few people in the halls and none of my teachers knew my name. But eventually, once I began making friends, the feeling of intense loneliness and anxiety passed. In the first few weeks I met a girl in my introductory political science course who insisted we join a sorority. Not having a clue what sororities were about, but being intrigued by the idea of trying something new, I decided to go along with it. I joined a group of ladies in the sorority Alpha Omicron Pi and the experience was fabulous. I was immediately accepted into a group of bright, friendly women of different ages and personalities. Soon I would not miss having someone to hold my hand through school and would quickly discover a new sense of independence. I realized I had entered a world where a note was not required for being late or missing a class. Suddenly no one really cared if I failed to submit an assignment, and best of all report cards were never sent home, resulting in no parent-teacher interviews. I was able to sit with my friends in the food court all day guiltlessly. I recall feeling quite relaxed about the whole situation and beginning to enjoy university. "So this is what freedom feels like", I thought. Unfortunately my calm quickly disappeared once I realized I hadn't begun writing any of my papers and I had three midterms just around the corner. I'm not certain if it's possible for a teenager to go into cardiac arrest but I'm sure I was quite near that state for the entire second half of that first semester. Obviously I had no clue what I was doing and my first set of grades reflected it. Following the winter holiday I returned to school relieved that I had not failed any of my courses, but embarrassed that I had passed only barely. I was fortunate enough to be in a sorority where one had to attain a specific grade point average in order to hold a leadership role within the organization. As a result, one of the older girls set up a study plan for me. I know that must sound odd, but the purpose of this regulation was to ensure the sorority did not interfere with our studies. Because of these women I was able to raise my GPA by an entire grade point by the end of the semester. Luckily, I would never receive such low marks again. It's obvious to me now just how crucial that peer mentorship was. These women weren't teachers sending a note home to my parents; these were friends that wanted me to succeed and provided me with the tools to do so. I had to be accountable to the organization. That might not suit every student but I wanted to maintain my leadership role. I wanted to help raise our chapter's GPA as opposed to dragging it down, and I wanted to contribute to this community of excellence.

This might sound elitist, but I didn't see it that way. The sorority accepted anyone who wanted to be a part of it, so long as the value of reciprocity was maintained. Those who received mentorship from the older girls were expected to provide it to the younger ones. I liked this system and I feel I owe many of my accomplishments to it. The sorority gave me my first taste of what it meant to get involved on campus. It was no different than an athlete wanting to be part of the football team. It meant working hard to keep up with my commitments.

First year was an emotional year: I wanted to get involved and make friends but I needed to succeed in school. It was an era of all-nighters and heavy coffee consumption, but most of all it was my introduction to finding life balance. I was simultaneously petrified and excited. Never in my life had the skill of time management been so crucial. I had to ensure I worked enough hours to pay for school, study enough to earn the grades I wanted, and set aside enough time to rest or go out, simply to keep myself from going insane. I had to learn quickly the skill of self control and motivation, which I can assure you, was a challenge at seventeen.

Second Year:
Thinking outside the box

"I used to have an opinion, and then I went to university."

THE BEGINNING OF SECOND YEAR was far less stressful for me – even enjoyable. I remember being excited seeing old friends and walking the familiar halls with confidence. At this point I had a general understanding of where all the different buildings were, and where to pay my fees, and I had a clearer idea of which courses I should be taking. I found second year quite comfortable for I was able to develop some ways of dealing with campus life. My situation was different from that of most other second-year students. I lived about an hour's train-ride away from the university so in the morning I had to pack enough things – food, books and maybe even a change of clothes – in case I didn't return until the next day. I was very much involved in activities such as sorority meetings or club events, and I even managed to find a job two blocks away from the University. I would soon begin spending more time at school than at my own house. What made me different from most other students is the amount of time I spent on campus. The University of Calgary is known as a "commuter campus". Because the population of Calgary is large and the number of students living in residence small, most students take the long trip to attend class and then often head home right away.[*] This means that few students become deeply involved on campus. I was different. But I enjoyed this lifestyle and was quite content with my routine.

My courses that year were more challenging than in the previous year, but because I had become more familiar with teaching styles and course structures, I didn't find any of them unbearable. As I began taking higher level courses I was becoming more exposed to class discussions and debates.

[*] Statistics show that in fact many 2nd year students feel more overwhelmed than first year students based on the amount of counseling and orientation focused on first years to smooth out the transition between high school and post secondary. Some believe that the heavy concentration on first year transition has made the second year transition even more difficult. As a result, in the US they are beginning to launch sophomore orientation programs.

I believe the major difference between first year and second year courses is that first year is about establishing a foundation to prepare us for what is to come, and simultaneously weeding out those not suited to continue. Second year, however, was filled with what I like to call "other side of the story courses". In these courses, I learned so much about so many topics that my world began drastically changing. Things I believed in high school to be absolutely true I now saw as mere perspectives. That's in fact the perfect way to describe second year, the year of perspective. And what I've learned is that with new perspectives comes more maturity. For the first time in my life I would be less of a stubborn, opinionated little girl and more of a speechless listener.

On the other hand, I should admit there were times when I felt a bit lost because of all the information that was being thrown at me. Because I now questioned everything it was hard to have faith in anything. We went from having faith in the one theory we had followed all our lives to being stripped of all beliefs and left with utter uncertainty. It leaves one feeling vulnerable. Nevertheless, harsh as it may be, this experience can do us good. I learned to say "this is one way of looking at it" instead of "this is the way it is" and thus allowed myself to become more open-minded and far more inquisitive.

I learned to value this new approach that summer in my first office job. I was hired as an office hostess; however, the interviewer decided I was over-qualified and would consequently get bored, and assigned me to an administrative position. My main responsibility was to prepare packages for our clients by verifying legal documents, making sure that they were correct in every detail. My newly acquired critical thinking skills came into play when I discovered that most administrators had their own way of preparing the packages, leading to inconsistency, and resulting in various difficulties. Noticing this, I came up with the idea of creating a training manual for the entire department, deciding on a single consistent method that everyone would be comfortable using. In general, I saw that the summer students were more flexible and adept at critical thinking than the permanent staff who were more experienced but less educated. The company offered to keep me on after the summer, but I knew I would not get far in the company without completing my studies. This was when I first began to understand the value of my education.

Third Year:
No more excuses

"It's normal to sleep at school, right?"

SINCE BY NOW I had gotten the hang of things, the third year should have been easier, but it was the most difficult. The work was far more challenging, my writing was substandard, and my grades were not good enough. My expenses were going up, and scholarships were hard to come by, as most were awarded to students beginning or finishing their degrees. I felt like the awkward middle child: everyone's attention was on someone else. I should have known how to study in order to do well, but felt ill prepared, and it was too late to ask for help, or at least I thought so. It was definitely a lonely year. I had to re-learn self discipline but at a higher level. My head was beginning to overflow with ideas and I was tired all the time. Third year was extremely challenging, but it is said that we learn most from our struggles; so perhaps this was the year of wisdom, learning about perseverance, endurance, and determination. Looking back, I think there were two significant developments that helped me finish the race: student politics – more on this later – and mentorship. I was lucky to take a course from one of the best university instructors, deservedly popular and the winner of many teaching awards. This man related all his lectures to life experiences, and through his teaching we became more mature. Living close to each other, he and I took the same bus, and during the journey he would counsel me and share his own experiences. He encouraged me to keep running in the Students' Union elections, despite losing two previous races. Eventually, it was his letter of reference that helped me gain my position there. Once involved in the Students' Union I was too busy to worry about my frustrations. This was the change I desperately needed.

Last Year(s):
What Next?

"Perhaps I should be a professional student."

I BEGAN FOURTH YEAR in a new role with the Students' Union. I had finally won an election and began my term as an external commissioner. This was an exciting year full of opportunities and I did my best to take advantage of every one of them. I seemed to get involved in everything and anything. I travelled to Ottawa to lobby the federal government on student issues. I went away for a weekend to attend a social justice conference with friends I had made in class. I organized campaigns to get students to vote in the provincial election. I even set aside more time than ever before to socialize at the campus pub on Thursday nights. It was exhilarating; best of all, it seemed easier than the earlier years. And in fourth year I finally seemed to get the picture: I did well, and knew how to keep doing well.

The classes were smaller now, and I got to know my professors and classmates. But what next? If I didn't win the presidential election then I would have to graduate; if I graduated I would have to get a real job; if I got a real job I would have to grow up.

A reflection

"So this is what my degree is for."

I HAD A RATHER UNORTHODOX ENDING to my degree. It turned out I was successful in the presidential election, which meant that I would be working at the university full time as the head of the Students' Union, taking just one class. As the SU president, I was required to play a dual role: the first was to represent 23 000 students, which demanded a great deal of listening, observing, and analyzing; and the second was to run a $14 million organization, which required me to think on my feet and make careful decisions. This was one of the biggest learning processes of my life. I've decided to highlight one lesson I took away from each side of my "dual role."

What I learned from students

In this role, I learned a considerable amount about what kind of culture our students were building. I also learned about how students are perceived in the outside world. I heard a great deal about apathy: "Students don't care, they're not engaged or involved . . . why don't they vote for heaven's sake?" And yes, I'll admit that I was often frustrated by students' lack of involvement, even in student politics. But the more I watched and listened, the more I began understanding what the modern student's culture was all about and it's not apathy. On top of a heavy course load, most students need to take jobs; and we are exposed to such a wealth of information that it's hard for us to share a single cause and to take a similar stance on each issue. So as a result, we've become selective on what we care about and how we care about it. In my time at the University of Calgary I have learned that students get involved in their own way. The truth is we do care – we write blogs, march on the streets and organize fund-raising. But we are diversified in our interests, so our activities usually don't make the news or get discussed in an election. And we do not always get support and encouragement from those in authority. I once attended a provincial election debate at the university between candidates hoping to represent our riding. At question time, I suggested that to get more youth voting, perhaps we should have polling stations on campus. To my surprise, the incumbent and eventually successful candidate responded by asking why they would make accommodations for us when we don't vote anyway.

What I learned from school

Part of my role as President was being CEO of a huge organization. I was required to represent students at the University's Board of Governors, and in meetings with the municipal, provincial and federal government. I definitely felt the benefit of my university education as I prepared documents for these meetings and took part in the discussions. In this job I had to use every ounce of knowledge or skill I had acquired over the years, because if I didn't I would risk affecting the education of 23 000 students. A scary thought to say the least.

In these circumstances, it seemed logical to absorb knowledge and take advice wherever I could. I was fortunate that my very last class provided me with a wealth of ideas for my work. It was a seminar on rhetoric and persuasion, and it couldn't have been more relevant to my position. We learned how people influence or are influenced by others in a variety of ways: we are persuaded by words, environments, music, pictures, colors, numbers and just about everything imaginable. I learned from this course how many elements are involved in the decisions we make – what drove me to make decisions for myself or for the student body. I also learned how to persuade university administrators or government officials to support me on an issue and to see things through the perspective of a student. And I learned to recognize when I was being persuaded or sometimes manipulated. I remember one particular class where we learned how powerful numbers can be. We tend to trust statistics, but we rarely ask ourselves what facts are missing or whose perspective is represented.

When we delivered presentations to our classes, we learned public speaking. When we did group projects, we learned to collaborate with people of different working styles. When we had to approach our professors or university administrators, we learned how best to communicate with people in authority. When we wrote papers, we learned how to develop strong written communication skills. When we attended lectures, we learned how to absorb information. When we had three finals in one week, we learned self discipline and time management. When we were taught about different cultures, we learned about our world. But most importantly I believe when we earned a university degree, we learned to persevere, to set a clear objective, and see it through to the end. And isn't this what it is all about?

The last thought I'd like to share is just how important educators are from elementary school to university. They spend hours with us and have a tremendous impact on shaping the people we will become. I can't begin to express the importance of the role they play. I owe a great deal of my success to the teachers I have had over the years. In the last few days of my term as president and simultaneously the end of my university experience, I was walking to my office and ran into the high school teacher who had advised me to go to university many years before. He explained that he and his wife had often read about me in the paper or seen me on the news. (This of course was a result of being the official spokesperson for University of Calgary students for a year). We exchanged words for a brief moment and the last thing he said to me was, "From what I've seen of you in the media, you've done quite well for yourself." I'm not even sure if he remembered that it was he who advised me to take this path; regardless, I am deeply grateful to him.

Looking back on what I have learned and the experiences I have had, thinking about the money I spent and the sacrifices I made for five years of my life, I know I can say with great confidence: *it was worth it!*

THE UNIVERSITY

The End of Boundaries
and the Constancy of Change

Dawn Johnston

I CAME TO THE UNIVERSITY OF CALGARY because of a brochure. It was the winter of 1997, and I was completing an Honours degree in English Literature at Memorial University in St. John's, Newfoundland – the city in which I'd been born and raised. I'd requested information on graduate programs in English and Communications from a number of Canadian universities, and was making the difficult decision about which programs were worth the steep application fee. With all the materials spread in front of me, I was drawn to the glossy black brochure from the Graduate Program in Communications Studies at the University of Calgary. Its cover was bold – a short block of text which said: "You are about to enter a whole new world, where old boundaries cease to exist and the only constant is change." I don't remember anything else from that brochure, or from the brochures of any of the other graduate programs. A whole new world – one which abandoned boundaries and embraced change? That was exactly what I wanted.

Twelve years later, with a Master's and PhD in hand from that very graduate program, and a thriving career in that very department, I'm pleased to say that the brochure delivered on its promises. At every step of my academic career, I've been challenged, pushed beyond my comfort levels, and forced to understand the roots of the beliefs and values – personal, political, intellectual – that ground me as a student and as a teacher. My experiences in this pedagogical environment have made "The University" (broadly defined) the place I want to work and live, and "The Teacher" the person that I'm proud to be.

The Teacher as Student

FROM THE FIRST DAYS of my graduate coursework in Communications Studies, I was excited about interdisciplinarity – a word that hadn't been in my lexicon prior to arriving at the University of Calgary. It was emphasized to me from early on that as a field, Communications had drawn from sociology, political science, language and literature, and countless other disciplines in the humanities and social sciences. What amazed me was the way in which my professors worked to bring together the best of these disciplines as they spoke to human communication, without any evidence of the disciplinary "turf wars" that I'd seen at other universities. My classmates came from as wide a variety of disciplines, as did my professors, and our varied backgrounds were treated as strengths in the problem-centered learning that was the basis in all my classes. Teachers saw the value of viewing the world from outside disciplinary boxes, and they taught me to do the same. When it came time to begin my Master's Thesis, I was fully supported in undertaking original research on queer spaces in Calgary, and was deftly supervised by a scholar who directed me to literature from gender studies, sexuality studies, urban studies, geography, sociology, and cultural studies. My supervisor encouraged me to inhabit a world without rigid intellectual boundaries and my scholarship was all the better for it.

I had learned to be an interdisciplinary scholar at the University of Calgary and I knew I had a great deal more to learn from the teachers here at the doctoral level. Once again, the principles of diversity and interdisciplinarity were valued; my supervision was shared by two professors; one in Communication and Culture, and another in the English department. They'd never worked together before, and came from vastly different intellectual backgrounds and cultures, but were keen to support my doctoral work on activist uses of mainstream media. They suggested – and accepted – reading recommendations from each other in order to best understand and inform my work. While graduate student friends from other faculties and universities complained about intellectual one-upmanship and committee turf wars, I felt that I was being "raised" in an academic environment of cooperation. It wasn't perfect. I was plagued with all the usual insecurities and small-scale traumas common to every graduate student. The difference was this: my supervisors – my *teachers* – never played on those insecurities, and they never acted to exploit them in one another. Years later, as I examine my own relationship with my students and teaching assistants, I am reminded of the support I received and I strive to recreate that for the students I mentor.

The mentorship – indeed, the professional "grooming" that I received – went beyond the classroom and my dissertation. When I first applied for my SSHRC doctoral fellowship, my proposal was circulated among no fewer than six professors in my program, each of whom provided me with thoughtful feedback. When, in the final year of my program, I had my first interview for a tenure-track position at another university, my Dean, within days, pulled together a mock committee to help me prepare for the interview. The members of my own examining committee, in preparation for my doctoral defense, each subscribed to the small, independent, gay television network that was the subject of my analysis, and provided me with close, carefully considered questions and suggestions that have become the model of my own examination of students.

Every part of my experience as a student informed the kind of teacher I have become. Indeed, the fact that I was taught so well is a significant part of my decision to build a career around university teaching. I understand that for the vast majority of students, the content they learn in university may disappear into the recesses of their memory once a course or a degree is complete. But the process of learning – the experience of being taught well – will stay with them much longer.

The Teacher as Student Advisor

MAKING A DECISION TO STAY and build a career at the university where I'd trained as a graduate student was not easy. Colleagues advised against it. They worried that I'd never climb the academic ladder by staying here. They warned me that it can be impossible to get the people who were your teachers to start seeing you as a colleague rather than a student. Their advice didn't fall upon deaf ears, but I resisted it. I knew that being a teacher in a research-intensive environment would be a challenge. But I also knew that as a student in that very environment, great teachers had the most influence on me. It was, of course, immensely stimulating to be surrounded by leading researchers and writers in Communications, but it was even more influential to be mentored and encouraged and challenged by teachers who understood universities to be all about the students. This intellectual community is where I learned about my field, about my work and about myself. I believe that there is space within a research environment to foster my own core values of excellence in teaching and learning. The constancy of change doesn't always require a different address.

I'd begun teaching while still a graduate student, and had, upon completion of my PhD, taken a full-time position at a research institute on campus, but when the opportunity arose for a full-time faculty position in Communication and Culture, I jumped at it. A unique new position was in the works, developed in part to lead the University of Calgary's newly articulated emphasis on undergraduate student engagement. Communication and Culture would have a new "Director of Students" – a full-time faculty member who would, in addition to a reduced teaching load, work in conjunction with the Office of the Student Experience to head up the faculty's recruitment, transition, and retention efforts. It was a perfect fit – in addition to the teaching about which I'd been passionate for years, I had the chance to develop and hone my "student affairs" skills, and to work directly with prospective students, first year students, and student leaders to make their university experience as well-rounded and successful as possible. The university and my faculty were committed to supporting the position, and to ensuring that our efforts to help students successfully transition – both academically and socially – from high school to university and from university to the work force, were no longer *ad hoc*. Student "engagement" was a buzzword, to be sure, but it represented some very real gaps in contemporary student experience, particularly on a commuter campus such as the University of Calgary. Very few of our undergraduate students are living in residence – most are from the Calgary area, continue to live with their parents and socialize with their high school friends, and for many, the university is simply the place they come to take classes. It doesn't represent a meaningful part of their lives, and many feel disconnected from their school. Studies of student success throughout North America have consistently shown that engaged students – those who feel like active learners, who are involved in extra-curricular activities, and who report feeling part of a campus community – are more academically successful students. And while many of the different support services on our campus, from orientation programs to career advising, work successfully to meet the non-academic needs of students, there remains a significant gap in students' understanding of the relationship between their academic experience and the rest of their lives. One of the primary goals of the Director of Students position was to bridge that gap, and to help students make sense of the role that university plays in their lives, both present and future.

University is a time of enormous change for many students – even those whose living situation may have stayed the same. Many students are moving from classes of thirty students to classes of 300. Students who have been closely monitored by teachers are suddenly expected to monitor and manage their own time and workload. And, quite literally, students move from being known by a name to being known by a number. For many students, the relative anonymity of university can sound quite appealing. But it can also prove to be challenging and often alienating. Students accustomed to being active in class discussions can suddenly find themselves in huge lecture theatres, taught by teachers who know nothing about them, surrounded by classmates they've never met. These changes are exciting, but they can also seriously derail students – both those who have struggled in the past, and those who have typically enjoyed academic success. It was with these changes in mind that I began a "New to the U" program in the Faculty of Communication and Culture. An optional, non-credit, informal program, New to the U was offered to incoming students in Communication and Culture as a way to support their transition from high school to university. In a small group setting (10-12 students), I met weekly with participants in a casual, non-threatening environment where we'd discuss topics ranging from research skills to time and stress management to effective classroom participation. For three years, this program began with a new group of students each September, with the intention of meeting throughout the fall term, and each year, at the students' request, we continued to meet for the full academic year. The participants in New to the U were diverse – some were extremely high achievers who appreciated the opportunity to pick up tips and advice from a faculty member; others were students who'd struggled through high school and wanted to take advantage of all the services that increased their chance for success in university. Some were extremely outgoing, and very active in extra-curricular activities, while others were introverts for whom, in some cases, this was the only time each week that they actually talked to other students.

It was this program that had the strongest impact on me, and made me feel the most connected to students. As these students successfully complete first year, second year, third year of university, I hear from them often – sometimes to ask questions about how to handle a particular academic situation, but more often, to report back on their successes and accomplishments. Many of them have talked about how helpful it was to have a "support group" or an "inside track" in helping them to succeed in university; some have talked very candidly about how close they were to quitting school and how much it meant to have someone watching out for them. All, to my dismay, expressed surprise to have found a university teacher who cared about who they were and how they were doing. It is surely a failure in our own "public relations" when students uniformly expect that caring and invested teachers will disappear at the end of high school.

The Director of Students component of my job has been immeasurably rewarding, and it was with great disappointment that I saw it disappear in the new administrative structure of the Faculty of Arts at the University of Calgary in 2010, when the Faculty of Communication and Culture became a Department. That said, I approach a return to full-time teaching with excitement. There is perhaps no area where I've seen greater change than in the classroom, and it is, without fail, the environment in which I feel most stimulated. I've had the opportunity to develop a wildly diverse teaching background in the last ten years. I've taught in classes ranging from eleven students to 310 students. I've lectured to first year students and led seminars with senior students. I've taught typical fifty-minute classes filled with eighteen-year-olds, and I've taught four-hour Saturday morning courses with the adult-student population of Weekend University. I've taught courses in Communications, Film, Women's Studies, and General Studies, and I've taught those courses everywhere from small seminar rooms to large lecture theatres to vineyards in the north of Spain. There are, perhaps, many teachers who can lay claim to such a diverse teaching history – but few can lay claim to doing it all within a single unit in a single university.

Continually redeveloping my teaching practice has not simply been an option within my academic environment – it has been a necessity. While colleagues in other disciplines have sometimes complained to me about teaching "the same three courses . . . AGAIN . . ." or being "stuck teaching first-years," I can't relate to their complaint because I am constantly stimulated by the courses I've been able to teach. And I find nothing more exciting than teaching first year students – they embody that same sense of possibility that drew me to Calgary – and to university teaching – in the first place. But my pedagogical challenges have gone further. I've participated in new course development through the creation of a group study program on the food culture of Spain, and get to teach "on the road" with a new group of students every other spring semester. I've been part of curriculum redesign for the Communications program, and have led the explicit syllabus design of our introductory Communications Studies course. And now, through the university's Project Engage – a project developed to help teachers of large first-year classes incorporate the best practices for student engagement in their classes – I am redesigning that very course in a way that marries the best of established pedagogical techniques with new technologies such as podcasts and social networking media. I've been taught and trained and mentored, as a teacher, to embrace that change, and my career has been better for it.

The Fruits of Engagement

Project Engage, along with other student engagement initiatives at the university, gives me a great deal of hope for the future of university education. One could certainly look at it cynically, as yet another effort on the part of the university administration to keep tuition dollars on campus. But cynicism has never struck me as a particularly useful approach to university education. I choose to believe that the university is starting to recognize and respect excellence in teaching. Project Engage represents the university's awareness that there are problems with the way that first year courses are taught, but also represents a desire to do better by our students. It looks at the principles of excellent teaching and successful student engagement, and finds ways to carry those principles into large class environments. For those of us who teach, the benefits and joys of small classes will never disappear, but it is also becoming clear that those benefits are not exclusive to the small class environment. Many of the most successful pedagogical practices employed in my class of twenty-five students can be employed in my class of 300 students – it's more challenging, yes, but perhaps even more rewarding when it works.

I may have been wooed, thirteen years ago, by the University of Calgary's claim to be a place without boundaries, where "the only constant is change." This claim, of course, speaks to the very idea of the university – perhaps The University, writ large. While in the day-to-day experience of the institution, we may constantly feel surrounded by bureaucracy, boundaries, and red tape, the classroom, and the intellectual and social spaces around it, remain those boundary-free zones which drew me here in the first place.

I teach as I was taught. I seek out collaboration. I expect and encourage my students to be active participants in their own learning. I value experiential education and see inter-disciplinarity as a core value of learning and responsible citizenship. I've been fortunate to be part of a faculty – and now, a department – that values that work, and that recognizes the importance of training students not just in a discipline but in critical thinking, social responsibility, and intellectual curiosity. This is the lifeblood of The University, and the responsibility and reward of The Teacher. Caring about our students – wanting to help them make the most of their university experience – isn't the same as coddling them. We can demand a great deal from our students, intellectually, academically, and ethically, but when we stop remembering that they are people, when we stop caring about what's happening in the rest of their lives, when we stop finding ways to help them see who they'll become and how they'll contribute to society, then to me, we've stopped teaching them.

The university of today is a different place than the university of my own undergraduate studies in the early 1990's. The technology has changed. The students are savvier. The Teacher has to be prepared to change too. Criticizing the environment – the bureaucracy, the technological distractions, the funding cuts – is part and parcel of being in a living, breathing organization. But using those factors as an excuse not to teach well? That's unforgiveable. If anything, the increasing challenges thrown at us in (and by) the university are all the more reason for us to excel as teachers. As much as it is my job to teach texts and methods and theories, it is also my job to deliver on the promise of excitement and challenge of change.

Getting Here:
Welcoming Students to the Research University

Doug Brent

*Recruitment materials display proudly
the world-famous professors, the splendid facilities
and the ground-breaking research that goes on within them,
but thousands of students graduate without ever seeing
the world-famous professors or tasting genuine research.*

The Boyer Report

I had absolutely no idea how little first year students know!

Seasoned academic commenting on his
first experience teaching a first-year seminar

Engaging Academic Culture

LARGE UNIVERSITIES often style themselves as "research universities" to distinguish themselves from polytechnics, four-year colleges, and other institutions whose mission is not to inculcate a culture of research. But this "research culture" that research universities are so proud of does not always trickle down to undergraduates. We comfort ourselves with the generally accepted (by academics) belief that good researchers make the best teachers. However, many students and members of the public think the opposite, assuming that research is what faculty members do when they are not teaching, and that it takes up time that faculty members could otherwise be spending on their students. In my darker moments I sometimes think the second view is closer to the truth. But regardless of which of these competing but largely untested assumptions is correct, I very much doubt that the benefits of being taught by a practicing researcher are automatic.

I believe that we have a collective responsibility to take a much more active role in making the benefits of being taught at a "research university" clear to our students, particularly at the undergraduate and most particularly at the first-year level. It is not enough just to tell them that these benefits exist. We must *show* them that they exist by creating a space for them to become "legitimate peripheral participants" (Lave and Wenger 1991) in the activities of the research community. Those of us who teach in larger research institutions must find ways of improving students' undergraduate experiences or we will lose them to institutions that offer better class size, a homier atmosphere, and other perks available at smaller institutions. In order to hold our students' interest, we need to help them experience first-hand the one thing we can offer them that other institutions can't – the *academic culture* of the university.

Engaging students is sometimes presented as a means of reducing attrition. In fact, I am more concerned about students who do *not* drop out, at least not physically, but persist for four years or so stockpiling knowledge without being particularly changed by it or developing the inquiring, critically aware minds that we like to advertise a degree as providing.

Engaging students is not the same as amusing them. Rather, it is a matter of helping them become members, however junior, of the knowledge-making enterprise to which the university – and ourselves – owe our existence. We are fond of lamenting the fact that so many students seem to expect to be fed knowledge rather than thinking for themselves. But perhaps they have this attitude simply because they have not had an opportunity to learn that they are they are capable of academic inquiry, and that it can actually be exciting to engage in it.

In my interviews with students while studying their research experiences, I often found that they looked back on their high school assignments with an air of faint surprise at how impoverished those experiences looked when regarded from the vantage point of even a novice university student:

> The majority of the papers I wrote [in high school] were Social Studies papers where you take a stance, and they give you a question and you just start writing and defend it. And so there wasn't really any hard evidence or research that you had to do, so I wasn't used to the idea of researching, going out and getting all these books and magazines and pulling it all together.

This impoverished background may not be as symptomatic of bad teaching as it is of the fact that students of high school age may simply not be ready for the complex engagement with ideas that university work demands. Certainly such would be claimed by cognitive psychologists such as William Perry, who argues that university students progress through stages of cognitive and intellectual development from a highly dualistic and authority-seeking stage to more and more complex understandings of how to handle competing ideas (Perry 1970; 1981). Students' progress through these stages is driven, Perry argues, by exposure to debate about increasingly complex ideas – the sort of debate that characterizes a genuine research culture.

Kenneth Burke provides a controlling image for the research process in his famous metaphor of the unending conversation:

> Imagine that you enter a parlor. You come late. When you arrive, others have long preceded you, and they are engaged in a heated discussion, a discussion too heated for them to pause and tell you exactly what it is about. In fact, the discussion had already begun long before any of them got there, so that no one present is qualified to retrace for you all the steps that had gone before. You listen for a while, until you decide that you have caught the tenor of the argument; then you put in your oar. Someone answers; you answer him; another comes to your defense; another aligns himself against you, to either the embarrassment or gratification of your opponent, depending upon the quality of your ally's assistance. However, the discussion is interminable. The hour grows late, you must depart. And you do depart, with the discussion still vigorously in progress. (Burke 1941, pp 110-111)

Although we are all aware of how much we owe to our participation in our own particular part of this conversation, it is easy to forget how long it took us to catch "the tenor of the argument." We must imagine our students as having just walked into the parlour. Before they have even hung up their coats, they are bewildered by the conversation into which they have walked, and have no idea where the ideas being paraded come from, or in what context they are uttered. They have no means of separating well-reasoned arguments from self-important puff, much less of joining in with any confidence. And it doesn't help that everyone is speaking a dialect that sounds superficially like English, but which seems less familiar the longer our students listen to it.

Burke suggests that they could catch the tenor of the conversation if they listened for a while. Doubtless they might, if they listened long enough, and if at least some of the guests had the courtesy to talk to them rather than over or around them. But how much more welcome might they feel if a few of the guests took them aside and introduced them to a few other guests who might allow them to steer the subject, if only briefly, to areas in which they had some interest and even a few scraps of prior knowledge? How much better still if someone took the trouble to explain to them some of the rules of the game, the conversational conventions that would allow them to step in without stepping on toes or looking like fools?

There is an ongoing discussion of the rules of this research conversation, and how little many students know about them, in journals dedicated to research and to academic librarianship. This literature sometimes uses the term "bibliographic instruction," but has increasingly come to use the more inclusive term "academic literacy." This term contextualizes the task, not just as learning how to retrieve information, but rather as learning how the entire system of academic knowledge works (see Lea and Street, 1998). For instance, Leckie (1996) reports a huge gulf between the information-seeking strategies of the expert researcher and the somewhat naive strategies of the average undergraduate student:

Do undergraduates have a good understanding of how scholarly sources are produced, and for what purpose? Do they understand why a textbook may not be considered an appropriate source for a research paper? Are they aware of where all those encyclopedia articles come from, and when one might best use them? Do they realize that the person who writes in *Newsweek* and one who writes in *The Annals of the Association of American Geographers* are two very different types of authors, writing for different audiences and purposes? Evidence is mounting that undergraduates have, at best, only a vague awareness of the answers to these questions, and have great difficulty judging the difference between types of sources, particularly early in their university education. (p. 204)

In mining this literature, I am struck by an undercurrent of anxiety and sometimes near despair among people whose lives are dedicated to making information not just accessible but also meaningful to students. Usually isolated from the classroom itself, librarians receive our students – if they are lucky enough to get a chance to speak to them at all – sent over to them from our classrooms with a smudged set of specifications for a "research assignment" and little else. In fact, when presenting at a First Year Experience conference recently, I characterized academic librarians as "despairing and desperate people," and received an unexpected ripple of applause from a group of librarians at the back of the room.

Overwhelmed by the nature of the ill-defined task and unused to the notion of a scholarly network, undergraduates tend to develop strategies that can be characterized as merely coping strategies rather than true knowledge-seeking strategies. Several years ago I conducted a qualitative study on first-year seminars to discover what the process of research felt like to students, and to compare their experiences in the seminars with their experiences in other courses (Brent, 2005; Brent 2006). I found many of my darkest fears, and those of the librarians I had been reading, confirmed. For instance, when I asked a student about how she went about researching *Oedipus Rex* for a Greek and Roman Studies course, she reported a low-investment strategy that she had imported from previous research papers at high school. Her thesis was that Oedipus has caused his own downfall. "I had come to that conclusion before I found my sources. Then when I went through the sources I found points that supported what I had already thought was true." In other words, she started with a thesis and then set out to find citations that proved it. Seasoned researchers are sometimes guilty of the same, but few of us would think of this as the right order of operations. However, relatively few undergraduate students have a good sense of what it means to plunge into an ocean of literature with many questions and swim about for a while before deciding on some answers.

I also discovered that students seldom follow citation trails. Only one of the nineteen students I interviewed reported having followed up even one citation. They began each phase of research as if from a standing start, turning to bibliographic materials to find altogether new sources without following up on the ones they had already found.

I believe that this is closely related to their attitude to their own citations. They are painfully, even brutally aware of the university's almost pathological attitude to plagiarism, and diligently cite in order to avoid being accused of it. However, none seemed even remotely aware that a reader might appreciate an accurate citation that would help him or her go to the library and read more in the referenced material. This may explain many students' chaotic citation styles – if they don't see their citations as being useful, even in theory, to a reader who might be genuinely interested in following them up, then why obsess over accuracy? But it also reflects their lack of awareness that readings connect – that scholars "talk" back and forth to one another in the Burkean parlour of the academic project.

If we want to welcome our students into academic culture, we need, first, to remember how long it took us to get where we are, and not to expect to be able to make high school students into accomplished junior scholars overnight. We can expect a slow, incremental process as more senior courses build on skills and insights laid down in more junior ones. However, there are a few things we can do to get the process under way.

The ideal environment for introducing research culture is a first-year seminar in which students explore a topic partly for the sake of learning about the topic, but much more for the sake of learning how to learn about a topic. For those of us fortunate enough to teach one, such seminars furnish a small island of calm in which one can truly concentrate on creating an atmosphere of inquiry, work with students one-on-one periodically, and concentrate on facilitating a process rather than trying to "cover" a vast body of material. Few of us are this fortunate, but my research into, and personal experience of, first year seminars and how they facilitate students' acculturation has yielded a number of insights which, in somewhat more modest form, can inform teaching in almost any environment.

1. Welcome library staff as equal partners in the enterprise.

Why not invite a librarian into the class, when students have begun to form at least tentative ideas of their topics and have some concrete questions that they can be helped with? Better yet, why not invite the students over to the library, especially if the library is blessed with a good teaching lab space, where students can wrestle with their information searches while you and a library subject specialist circulate? And consider doing so more than once during the course, as students' topics mature and their information searches begin to fan out.

If nothing else, this will give students an opportunity to put a name and face to the librarian who might otherwise seem a strange and somehow intimidating creature. It might help students feel more comfortable approaching library staff for assistance, and even to formulate questions that are more answerable than "Where can I find something about biodiversity?" If this seems as though it is expecting too much of overstressed staff, let me assure you that I have found librarians to be hungry for direct contact with students and extremely grateful to be included in the discourse of research that we create in our classrooms.

2. Take complex research tasks a step at a time.

One of the most important features of the first year seminars at the University of Calgary is the fact that students work on a single large research project, in many stages, over a three month period. One of my interviewees commented:

> The whole class was about that one paper and about research and [the professor] was always saying, "Okay well this is

how you research this, and this is how you research this." I mean we did a library orientation day, she'd have a day where we'd talk about drawing information from media sources, like films and stuff like that. And she did a whole thing on Internet-based research and everything like that. Whereas the other teachers, it was sort of just like, "Well this paper, we're only going to spend like a week talking about this paper." So it was all sort of like, "This is where you can get your sources, go to the library and that's it."

In a content-oriented course, there is less time for this amount of detail on the research process. However, there can still be time to break the process into stages, starting perhaps with some brief summaries of individual readings, then more complex explorations of the state of the literature punctuated by assignments requiring students to follow up citations. Only at the end of the process should they be asked to formulate a defensible thesis.

As an added bonus, walking students through the research process one step at a time reduces both the incentive and the opportunity for plagiarism. The student who copies or buys a paper frequently does so because he or she is simply not invested in the process and sees it only as a product that must be obtained somehow and handed in. A student who has been led step by step into the scholarly conversation on the subject will face the final task of pulling together a paper armed with an array of resources in which he or she has already invested time and energy.

3. *Start a research task by giving students an opportunity to do some exploratory writing.*

Exploratory writing can mean a lot of things. Students can explore what they already know about a topic before they begin researching it actively. They can explore their own interests related to the topic, an important first step toward focussing the topic into something manageable. They can explore their responses to specific articles, or to other students' writing. The important thing, again, is that exploratory writing be used not just for its own sake but as a way of getting students thinking actively about a topic that they will be moving into more deeply and more formally as the course progresses.

You don't necessarily have to grade exploratory writing. You don't even have to read it – you can just check it off as being done, and/or let other students read it. The pressure to read every single word our students produce can be paralyzing, as it can prevent us from assigning topics in stages just because the prospect of reading the output is so daunting. One of the wisest remarks on assigning writing has come to me from Joyce Leff, an expert on writing across the curriculum: "If you are reading everything your students write, they clearly aren't writing enough."

4. *If you can, make time to discuss the project personally with students early in the process.*

Typically, only a relatively small number of students make the effort to talk to their professors in person, and usually these are either the keeners (who arguably are the least in need of personal guidance) or the complainers who want to talk to us about a grade that has been already assigned. The bulk in the middle are too busy, too shy, or simply too overconfident to come to us early in the process when our intervention can help them get it right rather than merely explain why they got it wrong. Others simply can't schedule an appointment during our posted hours, which are generally brief and therefore guaranteed to conflict with the schedules of many students.

The ideal remedy is to take a week or so of expanded office hours, require specific students to drop by at specific times, work with them to find times when they can do so, and most important, provide an item for discussion – a proposal, a draft of a brief assignment, a study question, anything that is still in process as opposed to a final assignment that has been graded, returned, and thereby closed. If you have a number of small cumulative assignments, the interviews can be spread over the assignments, so that even if you can't see every student about every assignment, you can see every student at least once about something – or, if you have a large class and are blessed with teaching assistants, those assistants can.

For more ideas on how to make the research process more engaging and less alien, I can't recommend a better source than John Bean's *Engaging Ideas: The Professor's Guide to Integrating Writing, Critical Thinking, and Active Learning in the Classroom*. While not strictly a guide to helping students master research, the book has sections on helping students read difficult texts and assigning research assignments that foster real engagement.

All of this obviously takes time away from simple coverage of material. A common reaction to setting an inquiry-based agenda is "But I have so much to cover, so much to tell them. How can I take time away from an already crowded curriculum to cover even a fraction of what they need to know about the research process itself?" This is the reaction that I like to call "anxiety of coverage." We know so much about our fields of study that we can despair of imparting enough of it to our students in the few short hours we have with them.

It is important to remember that this despair arises precisely because all fields of knowledge are packed with more information than can be mastered in a lifetime, and that this information is continually expanding. Of course we need to give students a solid grip on the most central concepts of our discipline: new knowledge must be mounted on a secure platform of old knowledge. But instead of hoping to cram everything our students need to know into a set of lectures, we are doing them a better service if we give them tools to find out more of what they need to know by themselves.

Teaching a research-intensive first year course – one that is truly research intensive, in which you create many opportunities for talk about the research process and interactions with students as they are doing it, rather than simply handing them an assignment and sending them off to our despairing colleagues in the library – is a revelation that no faculty member should miss. Some parts of the experience border on the tragi-comic, such as the student whose cell phone rang during group discussion time and who not only answered it but began a long conversation, and was genuinely surprised when I said, "You're in class. Tell them you'll call back."

Other experiences can make us aware of things that we might otherwise not even suspect, such as the fact that many students have no idea that they can contribute to others' learning. In an early exercise I often divide students into groups of five, settle on a topic, and ask each student to find a source that bears on the topic and to bring back five copies, which they share and discuss. The first time I did this, many students brought only one copy. I leaned back in my chair and said, "Gee, now what are we going to do? The other members of the group don't have any materials to work from for the rest of the class." Sheepish looks were exchanged, pockets were dug in for change, and some students left and came back a few minutes later with five copies. I take this, not as a sign that students don't always follow instructions, but as evidence that they start with such an impoverished sense of their ability to contribute meaningfully to others that an instruction to bring copies to share is so counterintuitive that they simply can't hear it.

Rather than dwell on what students don't know at the beginning, I'd rather spend more time on what they know by the end of even three months of engagement with research. One student turned in his first assignment, a brief literature review, toward the end of September. He had misunderstood the task itself and misunderstood what he was reading so hopelessly that his review bore almost no resemblance to the document he was supposed to be reviewing. I traced his confusion back to a lack of a felt sense that a literature review is supposed to give an overview of the existing state of the conversation on a subject for the benefit of a reader who had not necessarily read the original works. He treated it as merely a school exercise designed to prove only that he had read the material. Likely because he didn't know what he was supposed to be doing, his organization, his sentence structure, and even his punctuation were also horrible. I could not in conscience give it anything but an F.

Usually I assume that a student will be gone as soon as they receive an F, but this student dutifully came to my office and listened to my explanation of what he needed to do. Perhaps because this initial assignment was so low-stakes (5%), he stuck with the course. His next assignment was also an F, but it was a much more high-functioning F, and again he came to discuss what has gone right with it as well as where he should go with it. This pattern continued, but he stuck it out, with each assignment suggesting a bit more understanding of what I was asking him to do. By the end of the course, he knew enough about how to research a subject that I was able to give him a genuinely earned B-. In the process, not only did he learn about research, but I learned, in more detail than I had ever suspected, how easy it is for a student to get things wrong when they treat assignments (naturally enough) only as ways to measure them rather than as ways for them to model scholarly behaviour. (I saw this student again several years later when he applied for the Honours program.)

From time to time, we can see student engagement run so deeply that it becomes life changing. One student's grandparents had survived the Ukrainian Famine in the thirties. She researched the period exhaustively, first from a historical point of view and then, by interviewing family members, from a personal one. She even tried (unsuccessfully) to access the archive of the Institute of Ukrainian Studies in Toronto — evidently they did not think that an undergraduate had sufficient status to be admitted. She described the experience as meaning far more to her than the average school project:

> I had a lot of personal emotion issues though because what I was dealing with was really horrendous. I really don't deal well with atrocities. But when I got my grandmother's accounts there were so many things I didn't know, and when it happened to someone you know I had a lot of personal issues. I'd start working at it, and I couldn't work on it because I was just too angry. I did not expect that at all. In the end while I had learned a lot and for me as a person it was important.

When a student can't sleep at night because of her engagement with research, the experience reminds us of why we are here. Research isn't just an abstraction. It can be a lived experience of finding out more about what is personally important. It is this experience, not just the knowledge that we have stored in our heads, that can be our greatest gift to students.

References

BEAN, JOHN. *Engaging Ideas: The Professor's Guide to Integrating Writing, Critical Thinking, and Active Learning in the Classroom.* San Francisco Jossey-Bass, 1996.

THE BOYER COMMISSION ON EDUCATING UNDERGRADUATES IN THE RESEARCH UNIVERSITY. *Reinventing Undergraduate Education: A Blueprint for America's Research Universities.* Stony Brook State University of New York at Stony Brook, 1998.

BRENT, DOUG. "Reinventing WAC (Again) The First Year Seminar and Academic Literacy." *College Composition and Communication,* 57 (2005) 253-276.

BRENT, DOUG. "Using an Academic Content Seminar to Engage Students with the Culture of Academic Research." *Journal of the First Year Experience and Students in Transition* 18 (2006) 23-54.

KENNETH BURKE, *The Philosophy of Literary Form.* Berkeley Univ. of California Press, 1941.

LAVE, JEAN, AND ETIENNE WENGER. *Situated Learning: Legitimate Peripheral Participation.* Cambridge Cambridge UP, 1991.

LECKIE, GLORIA J. "Desperately Seeking Citations Uncovering Faculty Assumptions about Undergraduate Research." *Journal of Academic Librarianship* 22 (1996) 201-208.

LEE, MARY R. AND BRIAN V. STREET. "Student Writing in Higher Education An Academic Literacies Approach." *Studies in Higher Education* 23 (1998) 157-172.

PERRY, WILLIAM G., JR. "Cognitive and Ethical Growth The Making of Meaning." *The Modern American College.* Ed. Arthur Chickering. Jossey-Bass, 1981.

PERRY. WILLIAM G, JR. *Forms of Intellectual and Ethical Development in the College Years: A Scheme.* New York Holt, Rhinehart and Winston, 1970.

The Dream Life of Academics and the Scholarship of Fantasy

George Melnyk

*There are things that cannot be uttered
within the university or outside the university.*

Jacques Derrida, *Eyes of the University*

EVERYONE DREAMS, including academics; their dream life is ordinarily excluded from their public pronouncements both in the classroom and in their writings. But they dream all the same. And one of the things they dream about is fantasy courses they would like to teach but can't for a variety of reasons. Among these reasons are the restrictive nature of traditional topics in their discipline, the requirements of the teaching curriculum, and contemporary student preferences, all of which configure the educational marketplace. Because of these and other strictures, such as the evolution of knowledge and new technologies, the academic is required to be current in the field and that requirement demands time, energy, and adaptive mechanisms. But the major pressure for conformity originates in the impulse to play by the rules and not to go against orthodoxy, which in the case of academe is determined collegially. The collegium that represents the collective power of those acknowledged to be knowledgeable both preserves and enforces standards. Collegiality is a superego that represses fantasies.

Many decades ago I was employed at York University as a tutor in a Humanities undergraduate course, titled "Ideas of the Irrational." What a lovely contradiction that title contained. Within it there was some scope to escape a few of the more common strictures in academe. It offered a hint of unorthodoxy. The course involved readings at a university level and it offered lectures, tutorial seminars, tests, etc. – all the accoutrements of academic respectability. However, the students drawn to such a course were a different matter. They were the human element – that unpredictable, unknown entity that had its own reasons for taking the course. Later I discovered that a number of them had had mental episodes and they were searching for a validation of the normality of psychological tangents. I was a young graduate student at the time and didn't know that I was entering a mine field. The only definite image I still have of the course was one day taking my seminar group to the fields surrounding York University to experience nature and "wilderness," which ended up at a barbed-wire fence and a railway line on the north side of the still small and developing new campus. After trudging through some wooded areas the students were faced with an unexpected sign of civilization. As some of its discontents they were disappointed because they imagined that they were some way out, escaping from the tentacles of civilization. I had planned this seminar experience to show the students the power of illusion, and fantasy and its constant interaction with the barriers established by norms and the constructed physical universe of which we are all an integral part. They learned that escape was an inner, subjective experience and not something that could be achieved externally.

The same can be said of academics and their fantasies. They are a product of the world in which they are fully integrated. The strictures of academic orthodoxy generate these fantasies, which offer the illusion of escape from orthodoxy, but it is only an illusion. Even if a fantasy course came to be taught, then it could only be done under the rubric of university requirements and standards. Its departure from the realm of frustrated desire into pleasurable fulfillment means it would have to become normative and recognisable as a course.

Daydreams of untaught courses represent personal discontent within the academic self, but they also represent that self's creative digressions, which arise from other interests or training that cannot be brought into play in the ordinary course of events. They can be said to be a gnawing libidinal presence, which wants to escape a singular scholarly identity. They are the courses academics dream of teaching, but don't. They remain absent from the public record and exist only as private thoughts. They cannot be brought to the gaze of others without being transformed into their opposite – a non-fantasy. As the inexpressible part of each academic's life they are as much a symptom of restraint as are disciplinary boundaries, collegial rules, and contractual demands.

Disciplinarity and its sisters, interdisciplinarity and multi-disciplinarity, are ways in which knowledge is codified and stratified. These broad categories represent the ongoing expansion of specialized knowledge and its compartmentalization/departmentalization. The aspiring academic is first taught to narrow focus and then is expected to teach a wide range of topics in a discipline, having, it is claimed, been prepared through study to take on most issues as they are dealt with at the under graduate level. The concept of fantasy courses is not about a young academic's desire to teach one's specialization within a discipline or a particular area of an interdisciplinarity topic or being forced to teach uninspiring topics. Fantasy courses must be repressed for various reasons: either they do not belong in the course of studies, or an academic is seen not to have the qualifications to teach them, in spite of having sufficient background to construct such courses. This does not mean that a specialist in 17th century English literature dreams of teaching Chemistry labs or that a mathematician wants to lead a graduate seminar in Nursing. It means that the literary expert in one national literature may have the capacity to teach a course in another national literature or that the mathematician may be able to teach a philosophy of science course.

As soon as a person accepts a boundary, then that person creates a desire to go beyond that boundary. Rules exist to be broken because they are insufficient to contain the totality of academic imagination and desire. The very acceptance of restrictions and conventions generates the need to express the excluded. This is not perverse. This is natural and omnipresent because the human animal lives more deeply in fantasy than in reality. The walls that academe imposes on its teachers become walls that one wants to climb, see over, and eventually deconstruct. A colleague was able to overcome this dialectical process by having his dream course realized, by pushing the boundary. Titled "The Big Picture – A User's Guide to Knowledge" the course invited students to unify different branches of knowledge, first in small groups and then as a whole class. The unity was conceived by them. My colleague described the process the students underwent as "an art form and like a dream . . ."[1]

The sources of these dream courses are within the self and its intellectual autobiography, which is different for everyone. Academically I was trained first as an intellectual historian with a specialty in twentieth century European thought. Then I moved from the discipline of intellectual history to the discipline of philosophy covering the same period. Obviously I was interested in ideas, their formation, their dissemination, and their impact on cultures. But when I found myself in academe many years later I began by teaching an interdisciplinary course in Canadian Studies because of my publications in the field when I was outside academe. Eventually my academic universe coalesced into my being recognised as a cultural historian with two distinct specialities – Alberta literary history and Canadian film history. I was able to translate my disciplinary training in history and philosophy into the language of cultural history. My attraction to the literary arts and to the visual arts was something that came from within. I read vociferously about cultural figures and their lives and I spent my non-academic decades involved in the cultural field. I married my practical experience in culture with my training as an intellectual historian to do work as a cultural historian and I used my philosophical training to write about film, which I first approached as a historian and gradually moved to philosophical interpretation.

One might speculate that the field migration I experienced allowed all sorts of dream courses to emerge from a frustrated subconscious. It did. As a late comer to academe I possessed a wellspring of private desire to communicate the unapproved. I did not have the opportunity to teach subjects of 20th century European intellectual history and philosophy, which remain close to me. Throughout the forty years since my formal studies in 20th century European philosophy had ended, I continued to read and make notes on European thinkers of the period, not because I had to for professional reasons, but simply for the inspiration about life and language that those readings gave me. After I became an academic, when I was in my fifties, my reading took on a note of requirement, but in most cases it was simply an instinctive desire to be close to the world I had come from intellectually and to which I remained bound privately. It came from the heart.

In 2003 I published a book titled *The Poetics of Naming*, which was based on my MA thesis in philosophy. A writer friend told me it was "unreadable," which I took as the highest compliment because that was its intent. It is a book that cannot be consumed, only tasted. It is the kind of text that allows me to create an exegesis on many of the words that form a single sentence. Even reading it aloud requires a dramatic slowing down and an articulation of terminology that seeks to impose major stops in the flow of even a single word. The book was inspired by the Heideggerianism of my graduate days, when the discussion of a few lines in a text by that thinker could take up a whole seminar. It was one of the emotional highlights of those now distant graduate studies, which suggests that dream courses are first and foremost inspired by emotion. Yes, I do dream of teaching *The Poetics of Naming*, but I never will. I would like to repeat that experience for my students but a text like *Poetics of Naming* doesn't fit any of the areas in which I am allowed to teach, nor does it fit any the programs affiliated with my interdisciplinary department.[2] It would provide graduate students with an exercise in the imaginative deconstruction of language, providing them with an experiential insight into the illusionary nature of language. The "unreadability" of the text would create a wall or barrier that students would have to scale to see what lay beyond, just as those students in "Ideas of the Irrational" came to experience the reality of there being no exit from civilisation. Ultimately those students and those who might take "Poetics of Naming: The Hermeneutics of Language and Illusion" would experience "a course" which they would slot into other course experiences, either positive or negative. But there is a chance one or two of them would be transformed in their understanding as I was to the extent that I kept reading on the topic for another forty years.

A dream course as something unrealisable becomes a permanent inhabitant of the private academic self. It becomes a secret that is carried inside. If it were to be "outed" then it would lose the qualities of desire, hope, expectation, frustration and resentment that it carries as a secret. Over time the dream courses have come and gone in my mind, not finding any formal expression. And they have been there since the beginning. Hiding them means that a certain part of one's authentic self cannot come out. One ends up feeling, perhaps solipsistically, that the world is somehow deprived of one's deepest emotional and intellectual energy because these fantasy courses are closest to one's heart. This repression of the private intellectual self seeps out in strange and unexpected ways – in discussion with a student perhaps or even as an aside in a lecture. Seldom does it come out in discussions with colleagues because it would then represent a personal grievance as opposed to the litany of agreed-upon general grievances that float about in the academic ethos.

Fantasy courses arise from the real social and collegial barriers that academics experience as "the thing that cannot be uttered in the university" according to Derrida. This means that most teaching comes to represent a rather superficial projection of the self, a simple conveyance of knowledge in which the intense self has been artfully sublimated. The only academics who can escape this bifurcation are the first-tier, world-renowned thinkers, who can pronounce on any subject on which they write. Their writings, once acknowledged as ground-breaking, become a self-perpetuating acknowledgement of intellectual greatness, at least until they are superseded.[3]

Derrida's Gaze on the Academic Gaze

ACADEME RUNS ON CREDIBILITY and legitimatization, which combine into a form of natural censorship of knowledge that cannot be placed in traditional teaching or scholarship. Derrida states emphatically that "the university is always censured and censuring."[4] Desire and censure are opposite twins. Desire requires restraint because it can become limitless and destructive. Restraint, however, generates the desire to go beyond the limits of what is considered legitimate. Where desire and restraint meet is in the arena of means or tools. If an imagined course is not allowed the means to manifest itself it is de facto repressed. Control over means is the sign of a system, and a system is a web of power relations. Academics inhabit and recreate the power relations of a university. The dream life that they carry within themselves and which they are called upon to repress must also be repressed in others. This is known as collegiality.

Dreams are highly rational structures with their own, often odd rules and unusual relationships. Their contents are seldom bound by the normal rules that operate in the physical universe. That universe is represented in them as functioning differently. They have a pseudo-rationalized structure, which is irrational to another system or power relationship of which they are not a part. When the potentiality of a dream course is realized in an actual course it becomes part of the real world. But as long as it remains a dream it has all the pleasures of a secret, which is known and treasured only by oneself. An Other that is unspoken and unrecognised may have no legitimacy or credibility within academe, but it offers certain internal delights. These include the hidden expression of one's inner thoughts, the affirmation of one's unseen identity, and the pleasure of masking a part of one's self. Because they have not entered the web of approval that flows from collegiality, these courses maintain a visceral authenticity that can be re-dreamed and re-fantasized.

How does a fantasy course become a real course? Most

often it does not. Occasionally the prestige of the instructor or the shifting sands of disciplinarity or student demand allows something unusual or different to appear, but this is a rare occurrence. Collegiality is a form of peer review that represents the collective wisdom or a particular stage of specialized knowledge that is imposed on the institution and its practitioners. In the abstract this sounds like a typical exercise in quality control or keeping up standards, which at a superficial level it is. But it is more than that. It partakes in the psychology of individual academic relations and in the wider socio-economic persona of the university as an institutional power. Take funding as a factor in legitimization. If an academic can get external funding for a program or an idea then she or he can take a shortcut to legitimacy and credibility. If the research funding is approved by peer review so much the better,. Even politically-sourced funds can be accepted. Money confers legitimacy and it is recognised by collegiality. If another, recognised authority such as the state or a private foundation is willing to invest funding in the instructor the project quickly receives the imprimatur of legitimacy.

In the academic arena of interdisciplinarity where I reside as a scholar, I am able to move across disciplinary lines with a certain ease. In writing a new book, *Film and the City: Urbanity in Postmodern Canadian Cinema* I was able to incorporate concepts from Urban Studies, Canadian Studies, and Film Studies. The publication of the book, which is dependent on funding, brings with it a legitimacy that enables a new course or courses to arise. It is an instant text available to students and the publication of the book by an academic press legitimizes the topic. But a course based on the book is not a fantasy or dream course. It is part of the ebb and flow of regular teaching and its gradual movement from subject to subject. It has its place.

But a course created for a marginal field such as Male Studies, which would emulate Women's Studies, could appear only if the university adopted a program in Gender Studies, which my university has not done. A dream course can come to life under various disguised rubrics but that means an academic must have an inventive and tireless personality. Through subterfuge one can transfer dreams to reality, but by doing so one legitimizes both the dream and the strictures of reality where it now resides. The dream course becomes transformed from being a personal and secret Other to being a public and normative Same. Its transgressive nature is deleted through incorporation into the academic system of lectures, tests and essays. It must surrender its transgressive desires to be legitimate.

One of the exciting aspects of fantasy courses and unrealized topics is the movement inwards toward a more originary self that they represent. Their subjectivity suggests the potential of novelty and originality. The repressed is a new narrative, a counter-narrative to the academic status quo. A good example is my dream course "The Poetics of Naming: The Hermeneutics of Language and Illusion", which would encourage students to explore their own autobiographical relationship to language. When I was a graduate student at the University of Chicago I took a course, for which I had not registered, that dealt with autobiographical narrative and psycho-history. In that course I learned how important traumatic reversal was in one's life, and how episodes that brought on new directions could lead to emotional healing. For me a new relationship to language was a key factor. I had always felt oppressed by language and working to overcome that feeling was part of my engagement as a writer. Words were weights that had to be lifted and every time I lifted them I grew stronger. Weakness and strength are not important concepts in academe, but they have a crucial application in the human sphere. The whole notion of power relations involves the simple categories of strength and weakness, both of which are relative terms dependent on circumstance and one's place in any hierarchy. If one can move from a site of weakness, however defined, to a site of strength through the manifestation of a fantasy course then one has increased the potential for original thinking, something students might appreciate. There is value here. However, fantasy courses are radical challenges to the conservatism of the collegium and their absorption into the fabric of academic teaching is one way of co-opting them.

A vital aspect of this transformation process is the concept of responsibility. Derrida says that the "minimal requirement of responsibility" is to respond, to answer, to react, to offer something.[5] A dream course is a response to a barrier and its repression is an acknowledgement of the power of that barrier to hold back, to keep hidden away. So what kind of responsibility does an academic have to dream courses and the process of making them real? First, the dream course needs to find its way out. It needs to be a legitimate response to something that is missing in the syllabus, an answer to a problem. How the academic comes to legitimize a dream course can involve numerous routes. Since this is not a self-help or how-to essay I will leave the imagining of such routes to every academic's power to strategize and move forward in the academic milieu in which they find themselves. A dream course as a response becomes a sign of responsibility or the ability to respond. By offering it publicly rather than keeping it private the academic takes a risk and challenges herself or himself to the rigours of academic teaching and its requirements. They must rise to the occasion that teaching demands and by this very act, which involves preparation and planning, they make something credible. By making the dream course real, they must behave as responsible or responding academics within the parameters that they know and work in. By bringing their private selves to the fore, they are moving out of a safe arena into a contested one, where they need to be strong, focused and confident. First students and then their peers now have something to get their teeth into. This means their identity has shifted toward a more responsive authenticity then they would normally convey. Derrida might say that the dream course is a response to a barrier that in turns calls the academic to be responsive. By being responsible the academic contributes a course to the overall corpus that is academic teaching and by making that contribution generates a dialectical response that elicits new dream courses.

A university reflects its immediate non-academic environment as well as its shared legacy as a school composed of four primary classes: administrators, scholars, students, and support staff. So a university like the University of Calgary, where I teach, reflects the corporate milieu of the city of Calgary and its socio-economic determinants. It also wears the academic accoutrements and speaks out of the standards of a thousand-year old university history. It blends the two results into a unique academic configuration that only it has. The same blending occurs for every university on the globe, which is moulded by international, national, regional and local forces and their histories. So dream courses should be considered as arising from specific and even unique milieus. They may be as portable as the mind of the academic who dreams them up, but they arise from parameters that limit their universality or applicability. I cannot imagine teaching my dream course at Harvard or The Sorbonne because I cannot imagine myself there. I cannot "see" the students or the faculty at these universities, so I cannot project my course on to these sites. I can only project them on to what I already know or have gazed upon. My dream course is not a universal dream; it is a highly specific one that finds its home in my own academic milieu, where I know how to make it fit. The dream course is a product of its time and place. It has a limited shelf life.

Jung and the Dream Course

Dreams are integral to the intellectual/emotional or rational/irrational humanity of scholars even though scholars seldom recognise dreams as contributing to their understanding. The person who spent a great deal of his research life seeking to understand dreams and making them intelligible was the European psychologist Carl Jung (1875-1961). His research into dreams was experientially based. As the founder of the theory of archetypes residing in the collective unconscious of humanity, he found symbolic meaning in various standard elements or figures found in dreams. Typically he would comment that the presence of water in dreams was "the commonest symbol of the unconscious."[6] This suggests that there is a symbolic element in courses fantasized by academics, but a symbol of what? My conception of a course that I know I will never teach symbolizes my desire to liberate myself from the strictures of imposed syllabi and course requirements. This conceiving can be either passive or active. It is active when it is done in a projective, rational way, but it is passive when the academic actually "dreams" the course as part of nocturnal dreaming. But even when the course is being imagined in a rational way and constructed to resemble "real" courses, there are unconscious elements in that imagining, such as the symbolizing mentioned previously, that contain a degree of irrationality based in the emotional history of the scholar. My concept of the "Poetics of Naming" course may seem very rational when it is explained, but it contains numerous irrational elements that are omitted in the rational explanation or justification. Jung claims that all ideas are based on "historical precedents" that combine with "primordial archetypal forms" to establish the true totality of intelligibility.[7] In the case of the personal unconscious, the "Poetics of Naming" carries my personal complexes, some of which are known to me and some of which are not. There is always a "water" or "unconscious" aspect to all rational effort, especially fantasy courses.

When I develop and teach a regular course in which I have a limited personal investment, I can display in it values, beliefs and other rational forms of thought that I publicly acknowledge, but when I develop a "dream course" that will never be realized I can invest a great deal more in it and its significance. In dream courses we find much more than the normative categories associated with public discourse. We find the instructor's complexes and also archetypal presences that reflect the collective unconscious. In other words, the dream course is riddled with symbolism.

If one considers this overly egocentric and solipsistic, then one is missing the point that dream courses carry within their potentiality a certain power that is lost or repressed or erased when they come to be realized in the classroom. That power is the power of inner meaning that they carry for the scholar. They seek to express the totality of the academic's learning, a good part of which is experiential. What I am referring to is that elusive and troublesome term – wisdom. *Poetics of Naming* as a text had its roots in an experienced mystical moment. Since mysticism has no place in academic discourse, except as a topic of study, the subjective experience of the text can be translated only into normative discourse. If it is not normative then it has a communication problem. In exploring a text that cannot be quickly read or digested, the student comes face-to-face with a barrier that represents a challenge. Overcoming that barrier involves the student having some sort of subjective experience that is authentic to that student. There are few courses that have the rhetorical power or the instructional emotion to change a student. And yet the power of such experience can lead to valuable texts. Without the mystical experience being wedded to philosophical studies, there would not have been a book titled *Poetics of Naming*. Without the personal guidance that comes from a seminar engaged with that text there is little likelihood of the student having a subjective experience that might propel her or him to their own textual creativity.

Creativity and personal engagement result from imagining dream courses. This is not often the case with accepted forms of learning. Being rooted psychologically in an unconscious rebellion against norms and the institutional and disciplinary superego, dreams courses become personal statements. They go in a different direction based on a scholar's own sense of authenticity, which has not been allowed to blossom in a traditional academic environment. They may be constructed on the surface as a typical course, but their underpinnings are radically subversive.

No one needs to suffer anxiety over inventing dream courses. They serve as a valuable outlet for suppressed parts of the academic personality and they emerge out of the autobiographical self. The fact that there is a strong personal element and an archetypal aspect to dreams makes them valuable to students who are seeking self-expression and self-understanding. They should be encouraged, and from time to time even allowed into the curriculum, where they can challenge and re-invigorate what is often moribund and weighed down by the orthodox fetters of tradition. Dream courses are necessary acts of rebellion that re-adjust the power relations in universities. They may not be uttered but they do exist, and that existence is a valuable part of every scholar's life. They are often holistic representatives of personal and social ecologies that redress the deficiencies in regular curricula. They provide an essential link between an academic's outward scholarship and their pedagogical fantasies. Fantasy is not something negative, but a tool for creating emotional excitement and meaning when discussing ideas with students. An unrealized dream course is a stimulus to the scholar to personalize their discourse. A realized dream course is a marriage of a covert unorthodoxy and an overt orthodoxy. This synthesis creates a path to generating new ways of expressing knowledge. Isn't that what universities are meant to do?

Endnotes

1 Private email correspondence. 8 July 2010. Ron Glasberg. The email concluded with the following: "The point of the dream is that unity does not have to be exclusivist. It can be an art form and like a dream has a plasticity that is open to all dreamers."

2 From 2000 to 2010 I was a faculty member in the Faculty of Communication and Culture at the University of Calgary which was the University's interdisciplinary faculty. In 2010 it was amalgamated into a newly created Faculty of Arts and downgraded to the Department of Communication and Culture.

3 The concept of first-tier academics comes from a simple theory that I have presented to my graduate students, which they find easy to understand but hard to accept. The theory states there are four broad levels of academic status. The first tier is occupied by thinkers whose texts have a global following. They are considered originating thinkers. The second tier is occupied by academics who comment on these first-tier thinkers' texts and so garner status by association with the first-tier names. They present themselves as official interpreters. The third tier is composed of those who apply the theories of the first-tier to a myriad of specific situations. The fourth tier are graduate students who carry the top three tiers on their shoulders and from which they must fashion their own intellectual contribution. I have found that these graduate students love to engage with first-tier texts, are critical of second-tier writing, and loathe third-tier applications. But I warn them that in the end most academics belong to the third-tier and that is their destiny should they become academics. A curious prophecy of self-loathing-to-be.

4 Jacques Derrida, *Eyes of the University: Right to Philosophy 2*, Stanford: Stanford U Press, 2008, 46.

5 Ibid. 83.

6   C.G. Jung, *The Archetypes and the Collective Unconscious* tr. RFC Hull, Princeton: Princeton University Press, 1969, 18.
7   Ibid. 33.

Night Thoughts from the Ivory Tower

Michael McMordie

THESE COMMENTS ON THE UNIVERSITY and my experience there are written from increasing distance and a widening perspective. The starting point was a brief piece written in 1998 for a Faculty bulletin as I neared the end of eight years as Dean. It was suggested ten years later that I use it as the starting point for this chapter. It could now be seen as a "Valediction to the Faculty of General Studies" because that Faculty (later re-named "Communication and Culture") has since been dismantled, its programs, students, staff and faculty cobbled together, along with the former Faculties of Fine Arts, Humanities, and Social Sciences into the new Faculty of Arts. My later experience and continuing pondering on the university as well as the need to set the original piece in context for new readers has prompted opening with some Faculty and university history and a closing discussion of the nature of the university and its management.

History

MY OWN UNIVERSITY CAREER seems to have paralleled a distinctive phase in university education in this country (and, it seems, elsewhere as well). This began with expansion and innovation, and closed with decline and retrenchment. The stimulus was the post-WWII expansion of education to accommodate new families and their children (the "baby boom") as members of the armed forces returned to civilian life. First came elementary schools, then secondary schools, with universities and colleges to follow. [1] Existing institutions grew rapidly, some added new campuses, colleges became universities, and entirely new universities were founded.

The University of Calgary, its roots in the 1905 Calgary Normal School, grew as the Calgary wing of the University of Alberta's Faculty of Education. With post-WWII expansion of education in 1966, it became an independent institution under its own board of governors. Well-supported by a forward-looking provincial government, the university had already in 1960 moved to a new suburban campus where it grew rapidly.[2] One preoccupation of the 1960s was the environment and its degradation, marked by the publication in 1962 of Rachel Carson's *Silent Spring*. Another concern was interdisciplinary and "general" education (a key document was the 1956 Harvard report, *General education in a free society*).[3]

These were important themes for the new University of Calgary. Led by Jim Cragg, an ecologist and head of Biology, then Academic Vice-President, the new university founded the Kananaskis environmental research centre in the mountains west of Calgary and, in Calgary, a new interdisciplinary Faculty of Environmental Design. The latter brought together scientists, urbanists and architects to teach professional degree programs at the master's level concerned with design to preserve and improve both wild and built environments. Its architecture program was, from my arrival 1974, my continuing academic base at the University of Calgary.

A second academic initiative followed closely. It was decided to disaggregate a conventional Arts and Sciences Faculty in 1975 into separate Faculties of Humanities, Science, and Social Sciences. This came with a move from a three to a four year undergraduate program. The additional year was conceived as a common introductory year, intended to give new students a chance to acclimatize and to become familiar with the opportunities before them before settling on their path to a degree. These entering students were accommodated in a new unit: University College. The College became, as well, the appropriate home for some existing area programs such as Women's Studies and Canadian Studies, which were seen as interdisciplinary and not appropriately tied to disciplinary departments in one of the new Faculties. In order that students pursuing degrees in these areas could graduate in them University College soon became a new Faculty, named General Studies, with its own interdisciplinary degree programs.

The idea of General Studies, or "general education," was never well understood locally. It had deep resonance for those familiar with earlier U.S. initiatives, notably at Chicago, Columbia and Harvard. These were well-known to the Faculty's founding Dean, Bob Weyant, and his Associate Dean, Marsha Hanen (Marsha followed as Dean in 1986); both had studied in the U. S. At the core of the academic program they devised were the two "Heritage" courses, in the history of ideas and culture, to be followed by all students registered for degrees in the Faculty. These required courses were far from easy options; they required active participation including a good deal of writing and speaking and were taught with great distinction by a number of faculty members over the years, supported by graduate assistants and some remarkable sessional instructors. At one anniversary symposium a former student observed that they were the most demanding courses she had taken, and the most rewarding.

General Studies and "Night thoughts"

MY CONNECTION WITH GENERAL STUDIES came when I sought a home for a new undergraduate course in Canadian architecture. Two colleagues and I had devised this because at the time nothing was available to undergraduates on the subject and we thought this an unfortunate gap in the university's offerings. My own Faculty was entirely committed to graduate level studies and had no wish to embark on undergraduate teaching. The new course was clearly interdisciplinary in conception, bringing together various aspects of architecture: an art with a distinctive history, the product of a complex professional and commercial matrix with important social implications, and requiring attention to advanced building science and technology. General Studies seemed a possible sponsor; the Dean and Faculty Council were sympathetic, and the course was presented, first under the Interdisciplinary Studies rubric, then incorporated into the Canadian Studies Program. This link to GNST as one of its (many) instructors from other Faculties, led to my service on various committees and Faculty Council. I came to serve as Dean from 1990 to 1998.

Through this period, university governance was still remarkably open. Full, often impassioned, discussion of academic matters took place in General Faculties Council (a broadly representative body, comparable to the Senate in other provinces). Academic Vice-Presidents were easily accessible, and in my experience a source of wise advice and a responsive sounding-board for new ideas. My two Faculties were among the university's smallest but this encouraged faculty members, staff and students to be actively engaged. Faculty Council meetings were often contentious: its members were deeply committed to the high quality and success of students, courses and programs but not always agreed on the best means to those ends. Life as a Dean was always stimulating.

My two terms also proved to be unexpectedly demanding. Abandoning earlier progressive policies the province was seized with the Thatcher-Reagan philosophy of governance, especially its elevation of the free market and private enterprise well above more moderate mixed economy views. Centrist conservatism gave way to something approaching libertarianism (at least in theory: as in the U. S. under Reagan, its application was far from consistent).[4] I came into the office in 1990 with the university engaged in a planning exercise based on either continued steady funding, or a moderate increase. Instead, the government decided to cut its support for higher education by 21%, implemented over three years.

It was this experience which provoked those earlier thoughts, from the spring of 1998. "Night Thoughts of an Insomniac Dean" revisited in a less than serious way some of the tribulations of life as a dean.[5] I reported the sleepless 4 a.m. musings, more frequent as my second term neared its end, that were a recurring experience. Visited in the small hours by a host of anxieties, unsolved (insoluble?) problems, overdue deadlines, impending crises, these night thoughts brought with them the spectre of moral paralysis and the temptation to despair. Dawn came (Young writes of "man's presumption on tomorrow's dawn"), the spectres resolved themselves into the usual series of tasks and obligations, amenable to some small steps, if not to final resolution. Strong coffee, conversation with colleagues, other productive activities continued the treatment. A good day brought a group of us together, contemplating the abounding ironies, paradoxes and hypocrisies as we reconfirmed our shared commitment to students and learning, to knowledge and understanding.

A great benefit of a Faculty with a Communications Studies program was close association with students of rhetoric. They among us seemed to be best equipped to understand our struggles with the world of affairs. Emphasis on the practical application of knowledge, as well as on context and style, balance the claims of seekers of abstract truths who too often in the past have assumed they alone speak for the university.[6] All of us are, however, faced with the unsavoury compound of shallow utilitarianism and narrow individualism that seems to dominate current political thinking. Universities are usually under siege, if not for what they are, then for what they are not. The siege may be well-camouflaged: more money to do this, or that; teach more profitable skills, find expensive treatments for diseases, make learning more efficient, support economic growth; but little support for the question why?, to what end? "It is not a trivial question, Socrates said: what we are talking about is how one should live?"[7]

It is not a question to be answered by a university education. It ought, however, always to be before us; it is implicit in most of what we do as scholars. It was at the heart of the study of moral philosophy required of all students in the old Scottish university curriculum. It is an unsettling, uncomfortable question, subversive of settled opinions and the prevailing social order. It may by some be conveniently lodged in a separate compartment, infrequently visited and kept well apart from the working week. Those who insist on its intruding into daily life are often dismissed by "practical" people as out of touch with real life. When it is pressed within a university, that is seen as proof that the university is an ivory tower. Was General Studies one? I hope so. The heritage courses, at the heart of its programs, pressed Socrates' question on the students. For many it carried over into their other work. Whether this is interdisciplinary, or trans-disciplinary, or meta-disciplinary is less important than that it happened, and still happens. It can bring together the many different enquiries on which we're all engaged, in a common space.

When I wrote as dean eight years ago what came first to mind were not specific issues, problems, failures, successes, but the broad, continuing issues still before us all. The credit for survival and some important successes through these years belongs to others – my role was more to support than to initiate constructive change. The staff, students, and faculty of General Studies were astonishingly creative, and more than willing to carry through good ideas by patient effort, well beyond the call of duty. It was a privilege to have been part of the effort and to have some experience of management in difficult times.

Management

THE UNIVERSITY THEN, and universities now, more and more resemble awkward and cumbersome survivors from an earlier age. They are ill-suited to cope with the demands and expectations of current times. Hutchins at Chicago in the1930s and Kerr in California in the 1960s caught something of this when they variously described a university as a miscellaneous collection of departments and faculty united (in Chicago) by a central heating plant or (in California) by a common grievance over parking.[8] When I joined the University of Calgary there still existed opportunities to debate matters more substantial than heating and parking, but councils and debates seized with such weighty topics as academic goals and principles later came to seem an impediment to efficient management by senior administrators, and increasingly they were bypassed or squelched.

This pursuit of management efficiency may have owed something (perhaps a good deal) to the desire to emulate the success of major industrial and commercial ventures. There seemed an irresistible fascination with fashionable business gurus (one president early in his tenure announced the need for 'one big idea' as proclaimed by Jim Collins).[9] Collins's precepts drew on his wide study of business enterprises. They were intended to capture essential features of outstanding business success. The president thought Collin's ideas offered a key to pre-eminence for the university, useful lessons for its management.[10] It seems unlikely that any lessons will be learned from the recent failures of many such enterprises. However successful universities may be at teaching and research they don't seem to be good learners, at least from business. It's a problem that afflicts not just universities, but also other kinds of public education, health-care, and other public activities where private providers may be keen to compete and some conservative politicians are eager to reduce if not eliminate public involvement. The unfortunate response is all too often to try to emulate private industry and to ignore or eliminate the differences. And, of course, it's not just a local problem. A writer to *The Times Literary Supplement* quotes an email from the Vice-Chancellor of Sussex University on his plans for closing some programs and reducing staff while "Our aim is to continue to invest in successful areas in the University and grow our income where possible." The writer asks: "Are universities really businesses? And if not, what are they? Are they to become forcing houses for the immediate economic development of the country and nothing else . . . ?"[11]

The president, following Collins as reported in the university

Gazette, announced the university's need for a "hedgehog concept." In a web interview, Collins described all "good-to-great leaders" as "hedgehogs." "They know how to simplify a complex world into a simple, organizing idea . . ." He identified Darwin and Adam Smith as examples of great thinkers, and evolution and the invisible hand as such ideas.[12] "What does it take to come up with a Hedgehog Concept for your company?" he asked.[13] Collins didn't attempt to apply his analysis to any universities. Despite the president's support, it's not at all clear that it could be. Certainly the idea of a university Hedgehog Concept is puzzling. What sort of simple, single, organizing idea beyond the truisms common to all universities could there be? Is this a useful way to think about the university? Collins acknowledges Isaiah Berlin's much referred to essay "The Hedgehog and the Fox" as his source, but however closely the idea as Collins understands it may have applied to Walgreen, General Electric, Philip Morris, and Remington, it seems a strange planning metaphor for a university.

Reading Berlin's essay again makes this strangeness clear. He explains his comparison:

> there exists a great chasm between those, on one side, who relate everything to a single central vision, one system, less or more clear or articulate . . . and, on the other side, those who pursue many ends, often unrelated and contradictory . . . These last lead lives . . . that are centrifugal rather than centripetal; . . . seizing upon the essence of a vast variety of experiences and objects for what they are in themselves . . . [14]

The former, the hedgehogs, include Dante, Plato, Dostoevsky, Nietzsche; the foxes, Shakespeare, Herodotus, Aristotle,

Goethe, Joyce. While any good university will number examples of both kinds of thinkers among its members, which better characterises the university as a whole?

A "single central vision, one system" might animate a small narrowly focussed institution. But a large research university, with a rich mix of undergraduate, graduate, and professional faculties, must surely be centrifugal not centripetal. To seize upon "the essence of a vast variety of experiences and objects for what they are in themselves" could be a founding premise for university teaching and research as shared across a diverse collection of faculty and students.

Calgary and other large universities with both professional and arts and science Faculties are necessarily multi-disciplinary. Much of their creative force in recent times has been interdisciplinary, transgressing established borders to find new approaches to old and new questions, along the way giving rise to new fields of study. Berlin's fox seems a better metaphor, and a more fruitful source of planning ideas. Although, as Berlin noted, the dichotomy can be pressed to absurdity, this is not a trivial or frivolous matter. The President thought it worth bringing to the Board, and *The Gazette* thought it worth reporting.[15] A conception of the university is a serious matter, particularly when significant change is under discussion, deep budget cuts are once again underway, re-allocation of remaining resources is inevitable. It might be argued, further, that the administration has no business indulging in "big ideas" about the university. It is, rather, the faculty and the students who deal with ideas; the administration should be doing its best to provide the facilities and support they need and otherwise keep out of their way.

Still, frustration with complexity and a desire for simplicity by the higher levels of administration is understandable. It is responsible for presenting the university to an external audience that includes politicians who have little patience with complex matters. The view from above might be contrasted with a view from below. Those actually engaged in learning: the teaching and research that are the proper business of the university grapple with the diversity and complexity of the world every day in the classroom, study and laboratory. Inevitable tensions and some confusion arise. If the university's political masters tend see education in terms of immediate rewards and measurable practical benefits, it can be a difficult and unrewarding struggle to argue for a broader and more subtle view.

This points to a second set of confusions: the diverse and often conflicting expectations the university is asked to fulfil. An immediate and pressing goal for parents and students is a credential that leads directly to employment on graduation. Universities seem happy to oblige, with grand claims of high percentages of students employed in their chosen field within a year or two of graduation. Other conflicting expectations arise from the universities' allegiance to conflicting ideals, as Alex Usher has pointed out.[16] One ideal is the small liberal arts college described in the early nineteenth century by Cardinal Newman planning a new university for Dublin; the other is the high-level research university proposed by William von Humboldt for Berlin. Most Canadian universities fail to be either.

Research itself is a major area of concern: institutional success is often marked and advertised by the large sums attracted to support research, from granting councils, industry or elsewhere. A further more diffuse expectation arises from a social and political role assigned to the universities: the preparation of its undergraduates for citizenship, well-informed, active and responsible participation in society and politics. Finally, and influential, there is an expectation that the undergraduate experience will be enjoyable judged by criteria that have little to do with learning. "The student experience" is investigated and ranked both by the press, in annual surveys, and also by the institutions themselves at the behest of government and for their own use.

If this view makes the university seem an impossible enterprise that is probably not far wrong. On the other hand, most of these issues are not new and yet the western university has survived, and even flourished, for nearly a millennium. It was never a simple project. At its inception it combined a disinterested pursuit of knowledge with preparation for practical engagement in the world: the church, medicine, law, the state. If the former seems often to lose out to the latter that was also the case in earlier centuries. The tension between the two can be a fruitful source of creative growth, especially if those promoting practical affairs are mindful of the need for inspiration and renewal that can come only from new knowledge and fundamental truths, however provisional these may be.

One distinguished writer's statement of "what real Western education, as opposed to mere vocational training, is about" bears directly on this:

> the constant exercise of the mind in discovering, appreciating and debating major thinkers and artists, past and present; the exploration of key moral, aesthetic and political issues; above all, gaining an historical perspective on our (very real) European roots, perhaps the most effective antidote to the current all too pervasive malaise of presentism."[17]

The Faculty of General Studies (later Communication & Culture) has now been closed. Ironically, Harvard has just recently (2009) renewed its longstanding commitment to general education.[18] With the end of General Studies at Calgary, enthusiasm for university education as a distinct and important experience in its own right seems also to have waned. An understanding of the university as a very special community driven by freely expressed curiosity – about the universe, the world, society – seems unacceptable to government and barely acknowledged by the administration. Its decline was acknowledged by the Provost in a discussion with emeritus professors in the Fall of 2009 but there was no sense that this was an urgent concern, rather, just that it was puzzling and probably irremediable.[19]

Instead, the crass utilitarianism of government policy has been adopted by the university, so that "return to society", preferably measured in dollars, is given as the important reason for support. Students come to acquire job qualifications, time-to-degree and other measures of "efficiency" are used to determine good use of the supporting fees and grants. Curiosity and curiosity-driven research are tolerated but treated as marginal, no longer celebrated.

How should the universities respond? It seems the best we can do is make the piecemeal adjustments needed to cope with immediate problems. Still, continuing attention must be paid to the larger issues and overriding goals of higher education. More candour from administrators would also be a welcome substitute for the anodyne pronouncements of presidents and "good news" stories churned out by public relations departments.[20] The example set by faculty and administration engaged together in confronting real problems while pursuing common goals could only be good for students at all levels, enheartening to the staff who make the university function, and a welcome public demonstration of the value (and values) of the university.

Endnotes

1   David K. Foot, *Boom bust & echo*. Toronto: Macfarlane Walter & Ross, 1996.

2   Anthony Rasporich, *Make no small plans, the University of Calgary at forty*, Calgary: University of Calgary, 2007, p.15.

3   Cambridge, Mass.: Harvard University Press, 1958.

4   For a useful discussion of the social and ideological context see Tony Judt, "What Is Living and What Is Dead in Social Democracy?" *The New York Review of Books*, Volume 56, Number 20 · December 17, 2009, http://www.nybooks.com/articles/23519

5   *Border Crossing*, Spring 1998, 1-2. Edward Young, *Night thoughts*",

6   "...the phantom of ultimate ethical truth...", Bernard Williams, "Saint-Just's illusion", *Making sense of humanity*, Cambridge: Cambridge University Press, 1995, p.148.

7   Bernard Williams, *Ethics and the limits of philosphy*, London: Fontana, 1985. Socrates' question appears in Plato's *Republic*, 352D.

8   Clark Kerr, *The uses of the university*, Cambridge Mass.: Harvard University Press, 1964, p.20. Kerr later wrote that "Colleges and universities (and, in particular, medical schools within them) are the most complex institutions in our society, much more so than corporations or trade unions or government agencies or foundations." Kerr, *Troubled times for American higher education: the 1990s and beyond*, Albany: State University of New York Press, 1994, p.42. In these papers Kerr notes such issues as faculty members' weakening sense of allegiance to the academic community as already of concern for U.S. Universities by the early 1990s (p.24)

9   James C. Collins, *Good to great : why some companies make the leap – and others don't* , New York: Harper Business, c.2001

10 The same President, when asked about his current reading, cited a collection of Peter Drucker's writings.

11 Gabriel Josipovici, "What are universities for?" TLS Letters, *The Times Literary Supplement* January 6, 2010

12 This suggests a seriously limited understanding of Smith's writings.

13 http://www.fastcompany.com/online/51/goodtogreat.html
"Interview with Jim Collins,Disciplined Thought: Fox or Hedgehog?"
Fast Company, October 2001

14 Harvard University Press,and Roger Hauseheer, London: Pimlico, 1998,
pp. 436-7.

15 An edited version of the interview appeared in the *Gazette*, University of
Calgary, October 21 2002, v. 32 n. 10, p.7 2002, with a reference to the
complete interview available at www.ucalgary.ca/oncampus. This web
document is no longer accessible.

16 "True Liberal Arts colleges are thin on the ground outside the
northeastern U.S. True research universities with limited responsibilities for
undergraduate education are rare, too; many institutions that seek research
university status obtain it by stocking up on undergraduates, skimming a
little bit from each one and plowing that money into top-end professors
and research facilities. All of Canada's 'Big 5' – with the partial exception of
McGill – fit this description." Alex Usher,"Canada's undervalued universities",
The Globe & Mail, Globe Campus, February 5, 2010

17 Peter Green, review of Robert H. Martin, *Racing Odysseus*, in *The Times
Literary Supplement*, no. 5546 2009.07.19, p.8

18 Introducing the renewed curriculum in September 2009, President Faust
spoke of extended discussions of the future of liberal arts education.
"Out of that set of conversations has come the affirmation of the notion of a
broadly based education designed not so much to fill minds as to open them,
designed to introduce students to the very breadth of knowledge and the
tools of judgment and critical thinking that can provide a path to it.
So in the deliberations of faculty about how a liberal arts education should be
structured, we came as a university to a reaffirmation of the notion of general
education." http://www.president.harvard.edu/speeches/faust/091021_
gened.php The original position to which he refers was set out in the
report of the Harvard University Committee on the Objectives of a General
Education in a Free Society, *General education in a free society*, Cambridge,

Mass.: Harvard University Press, 1945.

19 Alan Harrison, "What is Happening at the University of Calgary?",
    talk to the Emeritus Association, 14 October, 2009

20 For instance, the various iterations of "Report to the Community".
    The October 2009 version had as a continuing theme the slogan
    "A strong idea" with such banal offerings as "The Idea: Students do better
    when they are engaged in their learning". A welcome contrast to this cheer-
    leading was the reported statement of a UK vice-chancellor that "student
    experience at his own institution was unsatisfactory". 'I just think it is
    important for us to face up to the fact that higher education in the UK is
    under immense cost pressures, and that we have had decades of being asked
    to do more for less.' He admitted the student experience at his
    own institution was unsatisfactory, although efforts were being made to
    improve it. 'I am not satisfied with the quality of undergraduate education
    in the university," he said." Manchester University vice-chancellor Alan
    Gilbert from BBC News Saturday, 15 August 2009. http://news.bbc.
    co.uk/2/hi/uk_news/education/8198318.stm

Contributors' Biographies

Jo-Anne Andre is a Senior Instructor in the Department of Communication and Culture at the University of Calgary. Her research interests are academic and professional writing and rhetoric.

Dalmy Baez graduated from the University of Calgary in 2009 with a degree in Political Science and a minor in Communications Studies. There she served as President of the Students' Union in the 2008-2009 academic year. She currently works at the YMCA where she mentors immigrant high school students, supporting their transition into Canadian culture and exposing them to post-secondary opportunities.

Doug Brent teaches rhetoric and writing in the Department of Communication and Culture. His main professional interest is writing: how people, especially students, write and how they learn to write, both in the academy and in the workplace. He has published *Reading as Rhetorical Invention: Knowledge, Persuasion and the Teaching of Research-Based Writing* and numerous articles on writing studies and on electronic texts.

James Butler is originally from Newfoundland and Labrador, but has been on the road for over forty years. After completing an undergraduate degree at age fifty five, he immersed himself in graduate school where he began researching identity construction, attaining a Master of Philosophy in Humanities at Memorial University in St. John's. He is currently working towards a PhD in Culture and Society at the University of Calgary. His dissertation is an interdisciplinary exploration with the Mi'kmaq in his home province.

Ron Glasberg holds a doctorate in intellectual history from the University of Toronto. He taught at Mount Saint Vincent, Trent, and the University of Western Ontario before taking up his current post at the University of Calgary. The focus of his teaching and research is the evolution of fundamental cultural assumptions in the context of Western Civilization and how these may be structured to provide a holistic framework for understanding what might be called the 'big picture.' Glasberg has a special interest in linking those areas of knowledge which appear to be very disparate (e.g., science and spirituality) with a view to gaining a perspective on the vast territory that lies between these extremes.

Margo Husby, or Dr. Margo (as her students call her), is known for her enthusiasm both inside and outside of the classroom, whether working with students or playing with her grandchildren. She has become reacquainted with life on the student side of the desk while she takes courses in Social Work in order to become a better resource for her stuents.. She teaches Heritage courses in the Faculty of Arts, University of Calgary.

Dawn Johnston holds a PhD and an MA in Communications Studies from the University of Calgary, and a BA (Honours) in English Literature from Memorial University of Newfoundland. She is an instructor and the former Director of Students in the University of Calgary's Department of Communication and Culture. Dawn teaches in the areas of communications theory, critical media studies, and food culture, and particularly enjoys teaching first-year students.

Karim-Aly S. Kassam is International Associate Professor of Environmental and Indigenous Studies in the Department of Natural Resources and the American Indian Program at the College of Agriculture and Life Sciences, Cornell University. Dr. Kassam was previously Associate Professor in the Faculty of Communication and Culture at the University of Calgary, Canada (1995 to 2007). In 2006, Dr. Kassam received the Teaching Excellence Award from the Students' Union at the University of Calgary. He has also received Teaching Excellence Awards in 1999 and 2002. Dr. Kassam's objective is to seamlessly merge teaching with applied research in the service of communities. His research focuses on the complex connectivity of human and environmental relations, addressing indigenous ways of knowing, food security, sustainable livelihoods, and climate change. His most recent books include *Biocultural Diversity and Indigenous Ways of Knowing: Human Ecology in the Arctic* (2009) and *Understanding Terror: Perspectives for Canadians* (2010).

COOPER H. LANGFORD III is Faculty Professor in Chemistry and in the Dept. of Communication and Culture at the University of Calgary. He has also taught at Amherst College (MA), Carleton University (Ottawa), Concordia University (Montreal) and as a visitor at Columbia University (NY) and the University of Amstedam. He is a Fellow of the Royal Society of Canada and the American Asociation for the Advancement of Science. His teaching has been influenced by his experiences as a research administrator including as a Vice president at Calgary and Director of Physical and Mathematical Sciences at the Natural Sciences and Engineering Research Council of Canada.

MICHAEL MCMORDIE studied architecture at the University of Toronto. After a few years in practice and professional registration in Ontario, he undertook graduate studies at the University of Edinburgh, where he also taught from 1965 to 1974. He returned to Canada in 1974 to join the architecture program of the Faculty of Environmental Design at the University of Calgary. At Calgary he served a term as director of the architecture program, and as dean of the Faculty of General Studies from 1990 to 1998. He retired in 2005.

GEORGE MELNYK is Associate Professor, Canadian Studies and Film Studies, in the Department of Communication and Culture, University of Calgary. He is the author or editor of twenty-five books, including *One Hundred Years of Canadian Cinema* (2004), *Great Canadian Film Directors* (2007) and *The Gendered Screen: Canadian Women Filmmakers* (2010). He has just completed a manuscript titled *Film and the City: Urbanity in Postmodern Canadian Cinema*.

BRIAN RUSTED is an Associate Professor in the University of Calgary's Department of Communication and Culture. He teaches courses in Visual Culture, Folklore, Documentary, and Performance Studies. He is the past chair of the Visual Communication Division of the National Communication Association, and continues on the editorial boards of the journals, *Visual Studies*, *Visual Communication Quarterly*, and *Culture and Organization*. Recent research dealing with visual culture, performance, and place has appeared in *Cultural Studies*, *Text and Performance Quarterly*, *Visual Studies*, *Ethnologies*, and *The Theatre Annual*. Rusted has also been active as a curator and media artist with works exhibited at the Museum of Modern Art, the National Gallery of Canada, the Southern Alberta Art Gallery, and the Banff Centre's Walter Phillips Gallery.

CHRISTINE MASON SUTHERLAND is Professor Emeritus in the Faculty of Communication and Culture. Specializing in rhetoric, both theoretical and practical, she pursued research in the history of rhetoric, including three essays on the rhetoric of St. Augustine of Hippo. Her major research interest, however, has been in the history of women's rhetoric, in which she has published a number of essays. Her edited books include *Women as Artist: Papers in honor of Marsha Hanen* (1993) and *The Changing Condition: Women in the History of Rhetoric* (1999). Her single-authored study of the rhetoric of an early modern woman thinker and writer, *The Eloquence of Mary Astell*, was published in 2005.